THE COLLECTED POEMS OF TERENCE TILLER

The Collected Poems

TERENCE TILLER

EYEWEAR PUBLISHING

First published in 2016
by Eyewear Publishing Ltd
Suite 333, 19-21 Crawford Street
Marylebone, London W1H 1PJ
United Kingdom

Typeset with graphic design by Edwin Smet
Printed in England by TJ International Ltd, Padstow, Cornwall

ISBN 978-1-911335-40-5

Eyewear wishes to thank Jonathan Wonham for his generous patronage of our press.

Eyewear publishing wishes to thank the Tiller Estate and family for their advice and guidance during this project, especially Matthew and Verity. A special thanks to the interns and editors who assisted in the typing and proofreading of this manuscript, especially Rosanna Hildyard; and the designer, Edwin Smet.

FSC
www.fsc.org
MIX
Paper from responsible sources
FSC® C013056

WWW.EYEWEARPUBLISHING.COM

TABLE OF CONTENTS

THE INWARD ANIMAL (1943)

UNARM, EROS (1947)

READING A MEDAL, AND OTHER POEMS (1957)

NOTES FOR A MYTH (1968)

APPENDIX A: POEMS BY SARAH TILLER

APPENDIX B: POEMS BY MATTHEW TILLER

Terence Tiller (1916-1987), who was associated with the Cairo-based Personal Landscape group of poets active during World War II, wrote densely crafted, allusive, and profoundly sensuous verse. Born in Cornwall, Tiller was educated at Latymer School, London, and Jesus College, Cambridge. Following a brief period lecturing in medieval history at Cambridge, he spent the war teaching English at Cairo's Fu'ad University before returning to England to work as a prolific BBC radio producer and writer. His productions included the first radio adaptation of Tolkien's *Lord of the Rings* and a weekly chess programme, which led to the publication of his *Chess Treasury of the Air* in 1966.

In addition to six volumes of poetry, Tiller's published works include translations of Dante's *Inferno* and William Langland's *The Vision of Piers Plowman*. In 1980 he was awarded the Cholmondeley Award for poetry.

PREFACE

I wish I had clearer memories of my grandfather, Terence Tiller. Since he died when I was eight years old, all I have are some brief scenes. He taught me to play chess and encouraged me to get a chess computer to develop my skill: "Not so that you can beat it, but so that it can beat you." We played the piano together – if only I could recall what pieces... After I brought up an argument I had had with a friend over the nature of infinity, Grandad expounded on the subject, showing a mathematical erudition that I recognise in poems such as 'Luna'. But these recollections do not add up to the first-hand image that one might hope for.

Naturally, I was barely aware of his poetry while he was alive. As a teenager I skimmed through his books and liked an occasional poem ('Folk Song' stood out), but mostly found them off-puttingly incomprehensible. I went back to them now and then as an adult and found my appreciation of them gradually increasing, but it was only after Todd Swift's marvellous idea for this collection that I gave them the attention they deserved. Reading Terence Tiller's work fully for the first time is like meeting a new person. I am in the odd position of knowing my grandfather's artistic self better than I ever knew his everyday self.

The experience has been awe-inspiring. Each poem contains the original, perfectly evocative imagery that great verse should have, and I am immensely proud to be related to the poet. At the same time, I have had the sense that I am not always fully appreciating or understanding his work. Some poems I have no difficulty comprehending; some I have understood after researching the names or terms used; and there is a third group that I still find baffling. I mention this because I am aware that other people have had the same reaction. Terence Tiller acknowledges as much in the foreword to *That Singing*

Mesh: his references 'have their origins in (for today) an unusually wide range of disciplines'. Despite glossing some of the poems from that volume, he is unapologetic about how difficult they are, and rightly so. Perhaps by bringing up the question of how easy or hard you may find his work, I am underestimating you, the reader. I certainly hope so. But if you do find it challenging, I hope you will relish that challenge and feel it ultimately rewarding, as I did.

At Todd's suggestion, I have included some of my own poetry and that of my mother, Sarah Tiller. I have somewhat mixed feelings about doing this. I am very keen to share my mother's work with a wider audience than it had when she was alive, and it would be dishonest to pretend that I would not like my verse appreciated too. I hope that these poems will give readers a little extra enjoyment of this book. On the other hand, I want to make it clear that this book is about, and should be judged by, Terence Tiller's poetry. That is why my mother's and my own poems are here as appendices, definitely subsidiary to my grandfather's work, not equal.

Some background on my mother and her poetry: she was a shy, kind, loving, very intelligent person who for most of her life never had a medium to express all her positive qualities. She began writing seriously a short time after she was diagnosed with cancer. Partly because of those circumstances, her poems are much darker than one might have expected if one had met her. Yet there is also a lot of beauty and humour there, and powerfully vivid phrases. As with my grandfather's poetry, I hope that you will take pleasure in discovering what might otherwise have been overlooked.

MATTHEW TILLER

TERENCE TILLER'S LOVELY SHAPES OF RHETORIC:

AN INTRODUCTION TO HIS COLLECTED POEMS

Terence Tiller's poems, often explorations of love and desire, and early on set in Egypt during World War II, are almost the poetic equivalent of the Bogart-Bergman film *Casablanca*. Tiller, who is more or less a forgotten figure now, published three volumes with the New Hogarth Library in the Forties. *Poems* was the first of these, from 1941; his second was *The Inward Animal*, from 1943. His Third, *Unarm, Eros*, from 1947, completes a trilogy of wartime poetry arguably unequalled for its extravagant lyric modernism. Later, back in London he published three other volumes, if anything even more ambiguous, modern and esoterically erotic in manner.

One of the few contemporary critics to write on Tiller is Andrew Duncan, who emphasizes the sensitivity and sensuousness of mid-century poetry, especially Tiller's. Tiller 'seems to have devoted much time to writing poetry which was sexy and romantic'.[1] Duncan also notes his importance for future poetry: 'surely he points ahead to a whole strand of 1960s poetry which was reflexive and self-critical and preferred the fine to the gross'. Tiller also anticipates 'the concern with light' that 'appears in poets like David Chaloner and Denise Riley'.[2]

Speaking of sexy: Tiller, like Keith Douglas, insofar as he brought the twin tensions of mortal combat and Eros together – though with a far less murderous precision – might be said to be an influence on Thom Gunn, whose early poetry also explored, fruitfully, images of men at arms and love. This is a Renaissance trope, originally – one thinks of Fulke Greville's poems, such as 'Sonnet 78', with its martial imagery.

This is Tiller, but could be Gunn: 'All night they have been wounded on each other, / the waves that fall like armour from their poise' – not least because the tropes are ones we think of as quintessentially Gunn's – armour, wounds and 'poise'. Even the ending of 'The Child' has a characteristically dark, even nihilistic attitude recalling Gunn's early collections: 'The world in which we made you is not kind.'[3]

If Gunn was influenced even slightly by Tiller, and the many echoes are striking, this is yet another instance of a Forties connection to a Fifties Movement poet. However, rather more even than Gunn, it seems that Geoffrey Hill had been reading his Tiller by the time he came to write his first major published poem, the prize-winning 'Genesis' of 1952. The opening poem in *Unarm, Eros*, 'With The Gift Of This Book', ends with a couplet whose diction ('no myth will', 'blood') clearly echoes Hill's poem: 'No myth will ever come to any good: / but biting the wasp's apple; being blood.' The next poem in the collection opens with an image, 'the world / rolls' that again Hill seems to have borrowed for 'Genesis'.[4]

The point is not to score points here at the expense of Hill, a poet ripe with allusion, but to observe several things at once about Tiller's writing. It was very much a part of its moment, and embedded itself with many references to the key moderns – and aspects of this high modern lyric style, at its ripest fruition in Tiller, were borrowed and continued by poets as different as Gunn, Ashbery and Hill; and therefore it is plausible to suggest that the style has never, indeed, been entirely retired.

'Spring Letter', for instance, the second poem in the collection we have been discussing, is studded with echoes of other poets, some a little too near the surface to be completely absorbed.[5] I suspect Tiller did not think in those terms himself, and that, indeed, following the way that Eliot managed allusion in many of his poems, was aiming for a more intertextual effect. Some examples in this poem are 'the washed and choirboy afternoon' with its Dylan Thomas feel; stanza four includes the words 'body' and 'image', which were popular with Yeats, especially in his Byzantium and Apocalyptic poems. The same poem gives us the very Yeatsian 'awful beauty'; and a 'tigerish whirlwind', that feels an awful lot like Eliot to me.

All Tiller's early collections are, it might be thought, just a little marred by this fledgling tone whose imitative qualities are often very near the surface, where influence bleeds into homage or pastiche; but this can be read too as a poetic device. Gusts of Yeats ('sensual imaginings') and Eliot move in and across the poems, like sand across the Sahara. At the time, this likely made them at one within the modern lyric tradition and, perhaps to some readers, unoriginal-sounding apprentice work. However, after more than seventy years, simply the best of Tiller's poems exemplify the great end times of the modernist lyric.

Terence Tiller's work of the Forties was written during a time of personal and career crisis, when the young writer, wishing to have an academic and literary career in England, instead found himself trapped in Egypt. There, he formed associations with the *Personal Landscape* poets (associated with the expat magazine of the same name), including Bernard Spencer and Lawrence Durrell. Tiller was a teacher, not a soldier. Indeed, before his time in Egypt, he had been Research Scholar, Director of Studies, and University Lecturer in Medieval History at Cambridge. Like F.T. Prince, another great war poet of this period, he had to 'work twice as hard' as poet and scholar.[6] He was to find the fruits of his labours disappointing. When his funding fell through, he was unable to travel to Florence to study the research materials for his PhD thesis on late-medieval Pisa (the link to Prince's Italianate interests is noteworthy).[7]

Cambridge could only find him a position at Cairo, after his scholarship failed to be renewed. Tiller was not a public school boy. As such, he always felt somewhat socially alienated from those *Personal Landscape* poets like Durrell, who were so educated. This idea of alienation runs throughout critical readings of his work; indeed, his Egyptian poetry collections are quite Freudian in their sense of being *unheimlich*. The two key studies of this period and place's poetry, *Many Histories Deep: The Personal Landscape Poets in Egypt, 1940–45* by Roger Bowen, and *Personal Landscape: British Poetry in Egypt During the Second World War* by Jonathan Bolton, reflect the way in which Tiller and his poetry have tended to be considered posthumously.

Bowen's chapter on Tiller, 'Terence Tiller and the "Customary Self"', tends to the negative. Tiller (like many of the poets that came to notice in the 1940s) is held critically accountable for a lack of maturity, or even any later development. According to Bowen, Tiller, who lived in Egypt from September 1939 to September 1946, 'betrays little or no sense of change or adjustment'. Further, his poetry remains 'frozen, in an antechamber of experience'.[8] Perhaps even worse, Bowen regards him as the classic British snob, 'unimpressed by the cultural possibilities of Egypt's capital' – especially its bookshops – who never learned to read or write classical or colloquial Arabic though he spoke street Arabic fairly well.[9] This seems unduly harsh. I would rather read Tiller's acquisition of demotic Arabic to a competent degree as a sign of positive local engagement, rather than a turning away from local culture.

As Jonathan Bolton argues in *Personal Landscapes: British Poets in Egypt During the Second World War,* which reads the *Personal Landscape* poets from the perspective of Edward Said's *Orientalism*, it was not Tiller especially, but the British poets in general who tended to 'orientalise' the Arabs they met. Bolton notes how Keith Douglas found them to be 'unsavoury people' and observes that the Other, for Tiller, was not the native population of Egypt, but his own buried self, which his poetry explores the painful birth or rebirth of.[10] In this way, Tiller can be located within the personalism of the Apocalyptic movement, with its interest in private and mythic states and identities.

My own reading of Tiller does not dwell on his 'orientalist reaction' to Egypt as alienating, to his 'colonial disdain' or how he 'dispenses with locality'. I would like to note that, if Tiller is to be read as a lyrical modernist, and a precursor to abstract lyricism, then his tendency to base his poetry on a 'level of abstraction' is not entirely surprising, or uninteresting.[11] While Bowen may be right to observe that Terence Tiller was not a totally sympathetic visitor to Egypt, such an interpretation seems slightly over-determined; in expecting a direct empirical response from Tiller, relating his poems to the 'exterior' factuality of Arabic/Islamic culture, Bowen is de facto asking for a style that was not the poet's own.

Tiller was not a Thirties poet (in the sense of being journalistic or openly political).

Tiller, a young and sensitive scholar confronting financial struggles as the world battered itself to death, unable to leave a strange and remote city, might be excused for being a little overwhelmed. It would be nice to think that such a young man would have arrived in Cairo with the sensibilities of thirty or forty years later, but he did not – and his relative aloofness could be blamed on rather more private reasons than an ideology of cultural superiority; in fact, we know that Tiller felt socially insecure among his Western peers.

Bowen notes that one of his colleagues, Robin Fedden, considered Tiller the most formally astute of the poets writing for *Personal Landscape*, the one with the most metaphysical bent, the poet most dedicated to strict prosody and with a 'curious tensity of style'. It is a style that, in many ways, exemplifies an ideal of 'stylishness', a 'hybrid, joining Auden with Eliot' (as Bowen calls it).[12]

Tolley is another critic of Tiller's that has little good to say about his style, which he feels is borrowed from Empson: 'Tiller often proceeds as Empson did with a series of sententious phrases.'[13] Tolley feels Tiller emphasises the image too much, so that 'the imagery often takes over the poem'.[14] It is hard to see how a poem can be both too sententious and image-based at once (they are different forms of poetic argument). Tolley has problems with Tiller's syntax, too, and his general tone: 'The weakness of Tiller's less good poetry is its excessive obliqueness. There is an overelaboration of sensitive observation and the appearance of subtlety of distinction that is not sustained by further acquaintance. This goes along with a syntactical elusiveness.'[15]

I am not sure what Tolley means precisely by 'further acquaintance'. How long does one have to live with a Tiller poem to discover that its 'subtlety of distinction' is only a sham, I wonder? The 'overelaboration of sensitive observation' is another way of saying, as Duncan did, that Tiller is very sensitive and sensuous in his attention to his own self and to the world around him; it is exactly this passionate intensity that distinguishes the Forties Style, as I have elsewhere called it, and that I welcome.

As for syntactical elusiveness, this is another aspect of Tiller's style that is attractive – his lines are able to weave their arguments through rather complex contortions – as in 'Egyptian Dancer', to superb performative effect. Tiller's style – much like the great American poet, John Ashbery's – employs and enjoys the artifice of poetic rhetoric and expression to explore and display the meanderings of a sensitive, even dandyish elegance of intellection.

Tolley also quotes Alan Ross as observing in a review that Tiller is 'charming, full of grace' and like Donne. It is hard to imagine a poet so damned for his gifts. Tolley himself also notes the 'brilliance and coldness' of Tiller's work, and that it is 'impressively memorable'.[16] Tolley ultimately concludes that Tiller is a sort of figurehead for all that goes wrong at the end stages of full-blown high modernism, confirming my own sense that his poetry is, in fact, poetic modernism at its ripest apex: 'We seem to encounter one of the elements of modernism carried to the point of self-defeat: the life of the surface is over-developed, with the consequence that feeling is less effectively brought into focus.' Still, there is 'a parade of sensitivity'.[17]

John Press, poet and critic, in his *Rule and Energy*, also has ambiguously positive problems with Tiller. His poems are 'bafflingly difficult, because of their elaborate texture, the subtlety of Tiller's emotional perceptions, the darting, elusive quality of his thought, and the wealth of scholarship with which he loads his verse'.[18] This almost sounds like Eliot.

His best poems are those 'uncluttered by ornate trills, the argument not smothered beneath a profusion of glittering images'. Again, we see that the problem some critics have had with Tiller is related to his excessively ornate gifts. He is 'most successful when he keeps his eye on the object, and restrains his fancy from adventuring into recondite fields of speculation or into labyrinths of brilliant imagery'.[19] When he rules his energies, then.

Though unable 'to enjoy or even grasp the drift of much that Tiller has written', Press does concede that the poet has 'a formidable talent'. It may be that Tiller is not fully English: 'the poetic learning and the rhythmical complexity derive from the Italian and French elements in our culture and in our language' – making him sound, intriguingly, a lot like F.T. Prince, with his own 'Italian element'.[20]

It is hard to think all this profusion of style and intellect could be blamed on one man – brilliant and cold, a parade of sensitivity, sententious, image-rich, scholarly, darting, baffling, glittering, ornate, charming, full of grace – and one begins to wonder if what we have here is a failure of criticism itself at the period – a moment Tolley, Ross, and others could not conceive of a different style, another modern way, which was both emotive and aesthetic, engaged with depth and surface. In short, that this Forties Style of daring, glaring opposites, essentially fused in Tiller's work, rather than being praised for its originality and extension of previous modern modes, simply blows all critical fuses – and does not compute.

For me, Tiller's 1940s collections almost form one continuous and developing work, and, far from being frozen, develop across the books, while maintaining an unusual consistency of theme and concern. As is perhaps the most remarked upon aspect of his work, Tiller was interested in the 'inner animal' growing within the body of the common, smiling public man – in many ways, a personalized, Freudian myth borrowed from the rough beast slouching to Bethlehem to be born; in Tiller, it will be born in Cairo, close by, and the birth pangs are in tune with the world at war; in short, the neurotic conflicts in the personality of the poet result in the breaking through of a less ordered chaotic sense of self, or sensuousness. In the third collection of this wartime moment, this spiritual/erotic rebirthing is paralleled by the birth of a daughter, a striking emergence of an apparently biographical detail that also manages to imitate Yeats's daughter poetry.

Tiller is much taken with images of gestation and nascence – and his sense of the fertility within (and the struggle it engenders) is markedly influenced by, not only Yeats, or Eliot's reflections on sterility, but Dylan Thomas, whose 'narcissistic' reflections on womb and tomb so bothered Holbrook. Tiller is peculiarly taken with this subject, and his best-known poems tend to feature mirrors and doubled selves reminiscent of their expressionist (and symbolic) use in the 1940s films of Orson Welles (notably, *Citizen Kane* and *The Lady from Shanghai*). That Tiller saw films, and enjoyed film noir, seems evident from his longer poem, 'Detective Story', starring a heroine who looks like Veronica Lake.

Poems, published in 1941, is the most arch-lyrical of the three collections that form his Forties trilogy. A brief consideration of opening lines shows the diction and register: 'In the unloosed fantastic summer weather'; 'the instant splendour, the swung bells that speak'; 'they rode ahead of death on the strong turning'; 'Salt waters wash the oval fish, and flash'; 'Crouched in the womb I learned this fear'; 'Running to you, as the sad beast runs home'; 'Lovers have wept and been afraid'; 'All were lovely and with vivid souls'; 'Consider, metaphysical my heart'; 'The grecian tulip and the gothic rose'; and, in the collection's final poem, 'Now the night finds us; the bright worlds advance.'

It is not hard to detect the Yeatsian diction (beast, vivid); or the tropes of Eliot and Thomas ('wept and been afraid', 'in the womb'). Tiller is very much under the sway, here, of the modern poets of the 1920s and 1930s, as a young poet of the time would have been. What marks him out is, of course, that he is actually in the desert that Yeats had only imagined the rough beast slouching in, and his fear, though arguably metaphysical, has a historical cast to it – he was surrounded by a war-torn part of North Africa.

Even given his rhetorical precursors, his own rhetoric is always inflected with an urgency that ends up making his final collection of the Forties particularly impressive. Also of note is that Tiller's poems are – in rather contemporary fashion – not capitalised at the start of each line, but only at every new sentence (unlike, for instance, the work of Nicholas Moore). This allows for the elegant fluidity of the work to be displayed more effectively, and in this way he was ahead of his time, stylistically. Of the 1941 poems, one stands out, 'XX'.

The argument of this poem seems to be the following – lovers, confronted with the burial of a beautiful love object (death) have cried and been afraid; in the 'heraldic air' paradoxically the fictional beast the unicorn 'rages' very much immortal, as on the Grecian urn of Keats; beauty singes us in this ceremonial and artificial realm seemingly untouched by mortality.

Following the familiar myth of the unicorn, and as all poets of courtly love knew (and many weavers of tapestries), only a virgin maiden could gentle the fabulous beast and allow it to be captured, even slain. And so, either the virgin dies in pursuit of the tamed beautiful ideal (is deflowered) or the legend dies (chaste, ideal love); in the final stanza, we have the Yeatsian sense of the interpenetration of forces and things – the dancer and the dance are intermingled – and so too are the unicorn and the hunter-virgin – both are immortal – are, like the chevron of a 'sudden bird', a kind of phoenix event, perhaps (the unicorn was a symbol of the Incarnation). Chevrons were a key part of heraldic design; and used by the Spartans, those most warlike of ancient Greeks.

Tiller is fascinated by the tension between the actual, the body with its sexual force, its rage, its blood and desire, and the cultivated achievements of art and religious poise; or war and peace; or war, and states of truce, or amnesty. His Cairo was one such false oasis of Edenic calm, just before the arrival of total war, and so too was his outsider's Englishness a veil that drew him apart from the Egyptians he saw and met. His life, in study, work and poetry, as well as personal passion, was such a balanced tension between passion's sorrows and the consolations of aesthetic display; one thinks here of the Freudian aperçu that all art is born of suppressed libido.

The two immortalities are those of being painted (art) and dreamt (desired, imagined) – so that, again, this erotic, mythological relationship exists in several temporal dimensions beyond the daily. Art and dreams are not one, but two. We see, in reading this poem, the intricacy of Tiller's craft, and the thought behind the poems – where lyricism is put to complex and ambiguous work, employing expert knowledge of various fields. This is poetry at home with the heart and the mind, the passions and the intellect.[21]

Tiller's second collection, published two years later in 1943, is a further elaboration on these themes, and more. It opens with a brief foreword:

> The first and the last of these poems present (in a social and a religious mode respectively) the pattern of a personal experience that must now have been shared by many. The rest of the book is my own mode of this experience. Now that the war has taken millions from their familiar environment and associates, its impact and the impact of strangeness must have shaken, and perhaps destroyed, many a customary self. There will have been a shocked and defensive rebellion; reconciliation must follow; the birth of some mutual thing in which the old and the new, the self and the alien, are combined after war. This childbirth is not easy; the pain is sure to be there.
>
> For myself, and for many in the same or a worse position, I have tried to express the three parts of this pattern: the first distress; rebellion against place and circumstance; slow mutual absorption ending in the birth of something at once myself and a new self and Egypt. The 'inward animal' is this child, so unwillingly conceived and carried, so hardly brought forth.

This is a useful passage; it reminds us of aspects of the Forties that are in some ways strange to us now: the idea of a displacement of millions, so that a 'social mode' can address a personal yet universal experience of uprootedness; the religious mode; and the need to justify the recourse to 'personal experience' through contextualising it, historically.

The personal mode is still with us, and though it may be somewhat hackneyed now to use a trope of gestation to explore self-discovery, personal growth, and even more radical challenges to the inner self, the method and aims are clear. Taken in the context of postcolonial criticism of Tiller, this statement seems to excuse his apparent discomfort in Egypt. He admits to feelings of 'distress', then 'rebellion against place and circumstance' and finally 'slow mutual absorption'.

Tiller did not choose to be stranded in Egypt, strange to him and new, and it clearly, coinciding as it did with the war, overwhelmed him with its various sights and sounds. What seems admirable, at least to me, is how he sought to take these experiences and locate some order, some aesthetic synthesis, in them – not least because they were 'shared by many'.

At the heart of the collection lies a sequence of poems, 'XIV' to 'XVIII'. These five poems, given the stated aims of the book, explore dualities of image, reflection and self in terms expressly erotic and Egyptian (restaurants, belly-dancers) and also religious (Coptic Church). They form the midway of Tiller's Forties trilogy and warrant further exploration. One of the best known of his poems is 'Egyptian Restaurant'.[22]

This poem opens up a rather surprising dichotomy, or union of disunified subjects – for the poem begins in the image-conscious, visually fragmented and multiple mind of the poetic speaker, but turns its grounding to find 'one' who has the 'knowledge that he is' unlike the 'we' dining party the 'I' is part of. Both the I and the One are 'lost in a mist of mirrors as in tears' – but only the one knows the way out; the I is 'fleeting, plural' – lost in a 'crowd of jeweled ghostly Us'. Or maybe they – the we, I, us and one – are all equally lost in the trope of endless infinite mirrors.

This seems to me the best poem on multiplicity of self in relation to ideas of indeterminacy and observation (ideas brought forth by Freud, modern physics and Picasso, among others) that we have from the period – and it reminds me of the epistemological poem about the 'variousness of things' that we get in Louis MacNeice's 'Snow' with its 'drunkenness of things being various'. I also think, of course, of cinema, and especially Welles, who made divided selves and mirrors something of a specialty, though it may be Shakespeare in discussion with Banquo's Ghost that offers the textual basis for such thought.

This is not just a slice of life poem – a poem occasioned by a trip to a restaurant – and the diction veers between the precise and the precious, wonderfully: 'edges of acute refraction' sounds scientific; 'toss of beams' is more lascivious and gay. There is a desire, as we have seen, in some critics of Forties poetry, to always locate the moment the poet becomes ever more lucid and empiricist; this poem by Tiller is certainly concerned with observational data, but is not anecdotally simplistic.

It is followed by 'Street Scene' – the poetic speaker has escaped the seemingly infinite confines of the mirrored dining world of El Hati, and is now on 'Rue Soliman Pasha, Cairo'. Tiller does want the reader to appreciate the specificity of location, here – these poems are extended in space as well as time. The opening lines again show the concern with seeing and self: 'Down glittering rows the windows run / displaying you in shoes or books' – the 'you' being a woman whose 'silk and linen' is draped on 'a thousand simpering yous in wax'.

There is something disturbingly fragmented and reified about the female you that the poetic speaker sees, on this shopping street – for she is identified with parts of commodities – shoes and books, silk and linen. And she is cut up and divided into the suitably melodramatic 'thousand' pieces. At least, we might reflect, this you is partly made of books, a nice counterpoint to the potentially sexist 'shoes'.

In the last stanza, the poet becomes 'a maker-image too' as 'the passing images of you / along my busy street' affect him. In this sense, Tiller brings to bear the idea, in physics, that the observer alters the experiment. By observing the female love object, Tiller has himself reflected back in the myriad windowpanes, himself become an image-maker, making images of himself. And also, textually, his poem is a repeated image of the poem before, only now the we is an I, and they have escaped the interior mirrors, and found themselves lost without each other's real presences.

In the next poem, 'Elegy II', subtitled '*Shop Window*' [Tiller's italics], the theme is explored further. 'In the confused magnificence of love / is no community, but unsharing crowds / of shuttered faces where no secrets move.' Though set in Cairo, the poem also mentions the great London shopping street, Regent Street, and ends on a balcony above the bustle of the city described:

'[...] For he loves you still / who leans and weeps upon the window-sill.' We are a long way from Eliot's bored men leaning out of their windows. Tiller's emotionality is cinematic in its setting and its expressiveness.

The poem is odd for breaking into a rant halfway through – 'Never believe us; poets tell you lies: / the burglar breaks the window, and the door / blows inwards, and pictures tatter loose.' The argument here is a bit unclear, but it seems as if the poet is somehow being compared to the burglar, whose robbery has unexpected consequences even after having gone, leaving a windy house behind, that damages the art inside (art not worth stealing). It is trite to say that poets lie, and one wonders what it means in a poem that ostensibly ends with a poet weeping over a lost love.

This returns us to the muddled magnificence of the opening. Awkward syntax tells us that there is no community in the confused magnificence of love – only unsharing crowds. This is a paradoxical claim, and one worth trying to tease out. Love is not a public good, but selfish and crowded – it is, in short, neither exclusive or caring. We are in the midst of a love triangle. But also one thinks of the shuttered faces (of Muslim women?) on the Cairo streets.

In the second stanza, Tiller writes: 'Behind the dreaming shutters of our faces / the spider fingers thoughts, and we dissect / with sharp artistic hands our gains and losses.' One detects here echoes of Eliot's 'automatic hand' that puts on the gramophone. The faces, then, are the faces of the houses on the street, windows shuttered, but also those who walk those streets, as if closed to visitors or strangers. In this sense, the exterior and the interior again change places, mirroring each other in imagery, as Tiller is wont to do.

In the final stanza Tiller notes – and not without drama or complaint – that 'our delight will never be alone'. In this he is observing what Sartre said of hell – it is other people. Love, too, requires more than one person; but in such crowded places expect a mad bustle, not disciplined order; ardour is confused, but also magnificent. Or so the lying poet has found, weeping out over the public air.

In 'Coptic Church' that follows, 'magnificence' again is found, but now the duplicity is with the priests, not the poets, as Tiller discerns how 'the blazoned myth of Horus lies / within these faded images / where glowed Mithraic pigment in / the Thracian monks' symbolic line' – a splendid four lines. The image reveals images below, doubled up across time – religion is a series of identities interleaved, a palimpsest – 'the dust of worship in the wall, / the worship of ourselves in God'. Again, Tiller notes how the exterior – the wall – is within also (in God, ourselves) – or rather, how exteriorized forces and aspects (art, poetic words, performance) – reveal the inner depths they both seek to contain and also ineluctably release.

Release of the inner through outer performance culminates in Tiller's crowd-pleaser: 'Egyptian Dancer'. This topic was something of a shared pleasure among Tiller's crowd, as Bernard Spencer has a similar poem with the same title. Tiller's poem has not aged well, at least on the surface – a straightforward male gaze appreciating the exotic, erotic charms – the body in motion and display – of a foreign woman, being paid, as a quasi-sex worker, to entertain men – is arguably a little sexist. One wants to subtitle this poem 'Girls! Girls! Girls!' It is astonishingly explicit and erotic, for its time; one searches in any of Larkin (who presumably enjoyed such things) for any sensuous description of female sexual performance (or pleasure) as visceral; this is empiricism with gusto, well ahead of the Movement in some ways. Formally, too, it breaks refreshingly with more orthodox modes of syntax, dropping commas in rushed lines like 'and sweat breaks out she is bright as metal while the skirt'. Of course, we cannot help but think of Frank Kermode's work on the image of the dancer in this context.[23]

The dancer is, also, the poet, and the poet's poem. We have been warned that the poet lies. The poet also performs. The opening line slowly, with intention to tempt, sidles out, just as the line says the subject does. The drum-rhythm is the rhythm of poetry, and the ecstatic pulse that sees the dancer end in the darkness of 'past love', orgasmically drained, is also the text. Subject and text are one. But, as we know, it is also a poem of watching, and of lust, and of frank appreciation, so there is an onanistic, narcissistic sense of self-regard in the text – the text is turning itself on with its jouissance.

There are a number of striking phrases and images in the poem, disarmingly erotic: 'silver across the breasts'; 'coils on her own loins'; 'breasts are alive / and writhing'; 'the emphatic sex'. Her navel that 'winks like a wound' manages to combine a rather violent allusion to a vagina, and an eye – apt, since again, this is a poem about exterior and interior birth, the birth, in this case, of desire enacted, and desire fulfilled.

The second half of the poem gives us the 'half-naked body' – for indeed, the poem is half over. In the penultimate stanza, the opening word is 'Wilder' and then the colon indicates that that is also an order the poem is bound to obey.[24]

I now turn to a few key poems from Tiller's final book of the Forties trilogy, *Unarm, Eros*. This collection of thirty poems is introduced on the title page with a quote from the Yeats poem, 'Sailing to Byzantium': 'The unpurged images of day recede; The Emperor's drunken soldiery are abed; Night resonance recedes …'[25]

Tiller's typographical use of ellipsis here is a way of emphasising how both day and night recede after the evening revelry – how images of day, and night resonances, terminate. But not for Tiller, whose book, in titular fashion concerned with a martial figuration of erotic love – the love of soldiers, the battle of love – seeks to express and explore both the images and the resonances of days and nights in Egypt during wartime. As such, the poems occupy temporal occasions of blazing sunlight, or shade and darkness.

This preoccupation with the dual meaning, and implications, of the image – both as ocular, empirically-observed thing, and as romantic symbol (*pace* Yeats) – drives Tiller. In 'Substitutes' the 'private sadness' is squeezed 'until words / pearl; round it, and all images become / the private sadness and the life; and a name / blood'. The self's identity in language, the name, is made flesh and blood in a creative act that is half Mass, and half cleansing of a wound; the image of the words pearled around the squeezed sadness is almost physically gross in its implications, but also reminds us how the oyster dies when cut open to retrieve the pearl. The main point for Tiller is how the private myth, the self-story, generates, now, the poem – as it also did for Yeats, if not as explicitly. Tiller advocates 'going in and not around' – 'sucking the earth as wheat; become a field'. There is no substitute for being in the thing one writes of, for being that thing (much as Berkeley felt God put the heat into fire, the cold into ice) – the poet transcends myth by entering the mythic world, as an actuality: 'being blood'.

This idea is more flamboyantly expressed in 'Spring Letter', which makes clear the division between the poetic speaker ('me') and 'the world'; the world is not the 'more inward thing' of 'calm acres' and 'Mozartean air', or 'spring' – just as 'a wet garment on the body shows / the curl of limb and muscle, this day / droops in the shape of secret images'. The epistemology of this poem is a little unclear, but I think that the argument is as follows – the world presses like wet clothing on to a deeper (and stronger thing) – paradoxically, a muscular body, an ironic trope for an inner self, especially as that inner self is compared to air and spring – elemental aspects of calm; calm the world and its wartime violence ('the cold / indecency of outward violence') threatens.

In the poem's fifth stanza, Tiller explores this paradox of outer and inner connexion, these tissues of violence and order, of world and self, in terms of love:

> Love, and the lovely clothing of its play,
> its thinking film upon the flesh; the stride
> and ache of afterthought to our long woe
> our tenderness, the hangman of the blood:
> here in your flowered scarf of Egypt, deep
> as seasons under water, blooms our good.

This poem is Shakespearian in style – iambic, rhetorical and verbally playful – and, again, one sees here the Elizabethan impact often thought to emanate from Gunn by way of Yvor Winters.

Perhaps, though, we are closest to Herrick's 'Upon Julia's Clothes'. Tiller sets up a series of binary oppositions that align with his earlier list of what is of the world, and what of the self, or soul – a properly theological catalogue to be made in the desert: love/lovely clothing of its play; flesh/thinking film – so that the body corresponds to the Platonic ideal (love), with its flesh contrasted with the artifice above – the clothing, the thinking film, that plays like spume upon the surface. It is this artifice, this tenderness that hangs the blood – that holds the body at bay with its desires, another paradox. The rainy seasons, deep under water, bloom – the surface is sand.

Tiller's complex metaphysical conceits develop in 'Hands', which continues his use of tropes of love and vision, of language and what lies beneath. In it, we can begin to discern his poetics of sensuous rhetoric – that is, his equivocation of rhetorical forms, in speech and poetry, with shapes of desire in the world, and the inner self.

Readers of Tiller will be familiar with his counter-intuitive statements ('only the hands can love') that play with metaphysical wit. Here the argument seems to be, again, an inversion of the physical and interior planes of experience that borders on a Gnostic heresy – the transcendent world, the True, as it were, can only be located in the fallen world. In this instance, the claim is that, during erotic courtship, 'foreplay' and love-making, darkness shuts off the power of the eyes, and 'the lovely shapes of rhetoric', the visible signs of persuasive passion, the eyes, 'speak'. In short, the seductive powers of looking, and even kissing – emphasised for their verbal tropes of rhetoric and tongues – are failed orators, or courtiers, once the night comes and lovers are abed. Only the hands can locate and express 'love' – despite darkness being 'a girl-eater' that devours the sexual object – and pull desire from the abyss of pure carnality, into the firelight of 'learning and thinking' – for hands 'carry everything' – even bearing the girl up out of the darkness of sex, to somewhere altogether calmer (not 'the shouting of blood'). I am not sure this is a convincing argument, but it is certainly an ornate and clever one.

It introduces the secret image of these poems – a high lyricism turning – like a twisting, convulsed lover – on the bed of its own metaphysical making, fluently enjoying the paradoxes unleashed when poetry is both modern and romantic, as much Forties poetry sought to be – that is, personal, and mythic, in the Yeatsian sense, but also in a sense closer to an ideal of private myth. These are poems about rhetoric, using rhetoric to question and, indeed, enact the limits of rhetoric. They are performative. They perform their problematic poetics. One cannot accuse these poems of merely being stylish, even sentimentally so – for they are supremely stylish. They bracket style and seek to bleed it of meaning; the blood being ink.

This reaches its crescendo in a strange poem near the end of *Unarm, Eros*, 'The Phoenix Hour'. The Thebaid hours are likely those of desert monks in fifth-century Egypt in the Thebaid region – but also, in a brilliant ambiguity, the epic work of Statius (*Seven Against Thebes*), which was significant during the Middle Ages (Chaucer, Dante, Spenser and others borrowed from it). Statius' Virgil-inspired style was also, along with its martial themes of war, rhetorically sophisticated.

Here, Tiller fuses monastic austere devotion (Love with a capital L) with the rhetoric of epic poetry, and courtly love – in such cases, the rhetorical is the spiritual, artificial and devoted, neo-Platonic – the possession utterly, without 'ceremonies of sex'. There is a passionate verbal art, then, that poetry allows access to, which has the ceremonial grandeur of noble war and religious devotion, yet is unblooded by physical touch – 'wedded like rays' that are 'clever and bodiless'.

Tiller is on a search for a sun-cleansed ontology for love – one beyond a 'brittle fury' (one recalls in this the second stanza of 'The Wild Swans at Coole', and also the 'uncontrollable mystery on the bestial floor' from 'The Magi'[26]). Love might be like the phoenix. The phoenix, an Egyptian mythological creature, was based in Heliopolis, home of the Sun-God, Ra. The burning away after centuries, of this beautiful firebird, to release a new version of its exquisite song, promises a resurrection.[27]

In the First Letter to the Corinthians, Paul writes of Caritas (charity) as being one of the three greatest gifts, after faith and hope.[28] Caritas is a pure love, generous and without guile. 'Hysterica caritas mounting towards the voice' – an extraordinary line – seems to be an oxymoron much like 'terrible beauty' – in this case, an excessively emotional, panic-stricken love (belying Paul's claims for its serenity), about to emit as a scream, or cry of orgasmic exultation. The problem for readers of this poem is in identifying the addressee – is the poetic speaker on the verge of hysterical charity addressing a phoenix, a Yeats, a lover, himself as poet, or indeed, the poetic act or text itself? All seem likely, or equally unlikely. There is a sense of futility here – and I feel the argument underlying the poem (personal and mythic) fails to fully establish an 'objective correlative', as if the 'nothing else to do' – the dying fall of the poem – is both post-coital and post-scriptum. The poet cannot go on; the voice can do no more.

This is the paradoxical failure of Tiller's Forties Style – its 'marvellous' 'magnificence' is often clever and bodiless – a lyric abstraction whose brilliance is one step away from the dandyish irony of The New York School, in its excessively opaque diction. Yet Tiller is no poster-boy for Apocalypse. Indeed, when critics or anthologists have tended to favour his work they have hit upon his lucid Egyptian poems, of which there are several. Perhaps 'Camels' and 'Lecturing to Troops' are the best examples of a 'Movement style' born in the desert in the 1940s, far away from its ostensible origins in post-war 1950s Britain.

This poem, in diction and syntax, anticipates Larkin's style ('baffled a little, a little unsure'), but also contains Tiller's blend of tropes (bodily parts, faces, masks) and slightly ornate diction ('strange', 'supercilious', 'deliberating'). It is the acceptable face of Forties verse, perhaps – but again, not much like the war poetry of Keith Douglas.

One notes immediately the rhetorical repetition in both the first and last stanzas in lines one and two – geese twice, blind twice. There is no doubt a clever reference to blinds used to spot birds in this, but also the fact that the opening stanza opens with unlimited sky vision 'I see' and the last ends with a blind, or limited gaze. What this poem chiefly is, though, is a clear 'empirical poem' of the 1950s variety, using a regular stanza structure, rhyme and metre (more or less) to describe a subject, camels, with witty simile and metaphor, drawing a conclusion at the end.

'Lecturing to Troops' is one of Tiller's common anthology pieces, and is even more in the Movement ambit, with the troops 'wanting girls and beer' – and Tiller as a poetic speaker (he lectured to troops) feeling 'neat and shy'. One thinks of Larkin's awkward Church-goer here. The poetic speaker decides it is 'useless to be friendly and precise'. Further on, we get that reference to smut we know from Larkin: 'The strangeness holds them: a new planet's uniform, / grasped like the frilly pin-ups in their tent'.

I wish to end my discussion of 40s Tiller by noting his last poem of this trilogy of the Forties – his final poem in *Unarm, Eros*, 'Detective Story'. It is a strange, complex, mid-length poem in three sections; it seems too good to be true, but here is the quintessential Forties poem, in blocks of forties, times three, echoing his trilogy of Forties books. This is not entirely fanciful – the poem ends 'All this I read'. And the text itself is a cornucopia (no other word will do) of images, tropes, references, and merged and confused identities and confessions, as killers and victims each speak, taking on each other's voices. Indebted to the multivocal *The Waste Land*, but far more chockablock with references to mass or popular culture than Eliot ever was (except perhaps in 'Macavity the Mystery Cat') – 'Detective Story' is more Audenesque. It is the ur-Tiller poem.

I also say it is the quintessential Forties poem, if a critic wanted to locate one, because it effortlessly blends high and low diction, flamboyant themes and registers, is melodramatic, but also witty, romantically personal but also classical in form, and utterly forgotten now. I find it hard to imagine such a delightful, rich and clever poem – especially one about that most English of subjects, detective fiction – so overlooked now. There is surely no poem of the Fifties (save perhaps by Larkin) written in English that is any better, or more fun. There is a line in this poem, 'the final wonder of my disappearing' that we must surely be able to apply to Tiller himself. His own disappearance as a figure of poetic interest is a mystery, indeed.[29]

What remains, for a contemporary reader, though, is Tiller's exemplary fusion of emotionality and erudition, of personal expression, and a fearless interest in the ornate artifice of poetry, with a love of glittering image, the thrills and dangers of surface pleasures, and alertness to textual and psychic depths. Linguistically and intellectually daring, yet, indeed, sexy and romantic, Tiller is the sort of poet more poets might want to consider emulating, as they search for their own high styles at a time of political and personal challenge in the twenty-first century.

It is for this reason that I am so grateful to the Tiller Estate, and especially Matthew Tiller, his grandson, for assisting me in compiling what will surely, for the foreseeable decades, be the first and chief source of Tiller poetry for contemporary readers. That this book includes all the poems Tiller wrote, and had published, including from his many later books, is all to the good, though I have, in this essay, and up until now, tended to value his Cairo poems, rather more than his London ones. This bias is to be corrected in a later essay I hope to write on his later poems. Suffice it to say, for now, that my own emphasis is based on a love of the 1940s period, and is not a comment on the later poems' inherent qualities. Tiller was never a dull, and rarely if ever an inelegant poet.

In some ways his later career mirrored that of Louis MacNeice (another poet influenced by Yeats and Auden). Both poets worked as radio producers at the BBC; and both apparently struggled with various problems often associated with poets. Here the comparison needs to end, because whereas MacNeice has become taken up as a critical darling of many later poets (Heaney, and Muldoon, to name two), few if any poets of note have yet to fully endorse Terence Tiller. His work is an undiscovered country.

There was a time, when I was younger and hopelessly naïve, when such lack of recognition for poets I loved or admired stirred me to rage. *Oblivion?*! I was unsure what world this could be where such poems could exist without many, if any, admirers. Now, as I have turned 50, I recognize a more somber fact of literary existence: almost all poems, almost all poets, remain mainly unread, unrecognized, and unstudied, not only in their own times, but in those that come later. The myth of time as the great critical sifter is surely false. Time merely throws more poems and poets away every hour, every year.

Terence Tiller's greatest claim to fame now might be his work on the first adaptation of *The Lord of the Rings*. Tiller, born in 1916, would not have found 2016 a less stony ground on which to throw his witty, complex, stylish and often baroque poems of rich intellection and eroticism. Arguably elitist in terms of tone, purpose and design even then, 70 years later his poems, for all their glittering beauty, are in some ways as remote as the lurid gemstones of a bizarre planet we may never reach.

This radiant eccentricity, however, is the poems' true value. If we now try to read poems for what they give to our own sense of what we want the world to be, we will miss precisely the strangeness of other minds, other styles, and other visons, that by their very definition seek not to guarantee solidarity or confirm our solid judgements; but astonish, astound, and challenge us with their difficult otherness. New forms of critical study might want to begin to celebrate any poetics, any poetic style, that aims not to be at one with its society; but is alien, flamboyant, and self-remarkable. Tiller's current canonical irrelevance (he has been out of print for decades and is rarely anthologized) can in this way be read as an observable fact to be overcome with delight. There is arguably no better lesser-known English poet of the 20th century. What you have before you is quite simply a book of brilliant, different, things.

TODD SWIFT
Maida Vale, August 21, 2016

ENDNOTES

Sources Consulted

The text of the Collected Poems generally follows those of the first editions: Terence Tiller, *Poems* (London: Hogarth Press, 1941), *The Inward Animal* (London: Hogarth Press, 1943), *Unarm, Eros* (London: Hogarth Press, 1947), *Reading A Medal, And Other Poems* (London: Hogarth Press, 1957), *Notes For A Myth* (Chatto & Windus, 1968) and *That Singing Mesh, And Other Poems* (Chatto & Windus, 1979).

Some silent emendations have been made by Matthew Tiller, in accordance with Terence Tiller's corrections inscribed onto the published books in his own hand. Tiller's changeable spelling of Arcadian and other eccentricities of typography have been maintained at the risk of appearing erratic.

1 Duncan, *Origins of the Underground*, p. 17.
2 Duncan, p. 21.
3 Terence Tiller, *Unarm, Eros* (London: Hogarth Press, 1947), p. 48.
4 'Genesis' is collected in Geoffrey Hill, *For the Unfallen: Poems 1952–1958* (London: Andre Deutsch, 1959) but had appeared as early as 1952 in a Fantasy Press anthology from Oxford.
5 Tiller, *Unarm, Eros*, pp. 11–13.
6 Roger Bowen, *Many Histories Deep: The Personal Landscape Poets in Egypt, 1940–45* (Cranbury, NJ: Associated University Presses, 1995), p. 95.
7 Bowen, p. 96.
8 Bowen, p. 95.
9 Bowen, p. 97.
10 Jonathan Bolton, *Personal Landscapes: British Poets in Egypt During the Second World War* (New York: Saint Martin's Press, 1997), pp. 53–58.
11 Bowen, p. 102.
12 Bowen, p. 113.
13 Tolley, *Poetry of the Forties*, p. 50.
14 Tolley, p. 50.
15 Tolley, p. 50.
16 Tolley, p. 51.
17 Tolley, p. 52.
18 John Press, *Rule and Energy: Trends in British Poetry Since the Second World War* (London: Oxford University Press, 1963), p. 216.
19 Press, p. 217.
20 Press, p. 220.
21 Terence Tiller, *Poems* (London: Hogarth Press, 1941).
22 Bernard Spencer has a poem of the same title; and one also titled 'Egyptian Dancer' – suggesting mutual influence and discussion among the *Personal Landscape* group.
23 See Frank Kermode, *The Romantic Image*.
24 Terence Tiller, *The Inward Animal* (London: Hogarth Press, 1943).
25 Yeats, *Collected Poems*, p. 267.
26 Yeats, p. 181.
27 Wilhelm Max Müller, *Egyptian Mythology* (Whitefish: Kessinger Publishing, 2004), p. 31.
28 I Corinthians 13.
29 Terence Tiller, *Unarm, Eros*.

POEMS

(1941)

FOR DOREEN

Time is the medium, not the kind,
of dreaming in the actual tense;
under the dreams you will not find
their being, but their imminence.
Mortality is our defence;
we ask no marathon of mind
– building an amber about sense,
biting no future past the rind.
We only know the aloof design:
we shall not catch the running air
whose knowledge is the flight of birds.
Then take this written mask of mine:
all our instinctive deaths declare
the strange antiquity of words.

I

You will not see the sorrow of no time.
There will be birds bearing rings, ravens; hands
with an empty hourglass and a sword.
Things half-seen in a familiar room
will rise against you. These will be dangerous friends.
You will not see the sorrow of no time
or singing burst your melancholy cord.

In days of nightingales, and when our streets
are all nostalgic turnings, and the west
a broken harbour, there will be terror walking.
You will not know the crossing of our hearts,
the final stake that burrows through the breast.
The cruel delicious voices of the birds
will be silent for you. For you unwaking.

Then all my journeys will be bellman-like,
a wanderer in your city crying hours.
Call me the raven friend: that cry will come.
There will be nothing in the opened book
but evil spoken. These are the hollowed years.
Death in the longing way begins to walk.

You will not see the sorrow of time.

II

ODE

I

The time and the attainments dare not stay:
still from our lovesick arms the years break free,
and our deciduous passions stripped away
the gnashing axes fall. Like a tree
ambition rusts, and each remembered year
gathers about us. So for enslavement we
have won from earth the scent of juniper.

We who have sheltered in the pomp of steel,
agelong magnificence of worldly things,
find all our eagerness called back to heel,
time like a canker on the face of kings.
Now is the season of remote surrender
– the peacock flash, the winds' destructive wings,
and the loud epinikion of thunder.

A victory descending, but not ours:
the world's a wild unhappy little town,
but we that mutter against its emperors
have never leapt and plucked the eagles down.
We dream of bitterness, we defy from walls;
shelter, shut out with stone or diamond
the terrible greenwood where the lightning falls.

Cagers of winds, the warders of concealment,
are dying in Avilion with the knightly dead:
nor from their ashes rises up fulfilment,
but only shivering trumpets and the gold
wound-freezing water, and the moon in the mere
– cold weather and a belly full of blood.
And Robin my soul, what fools we mortals are.

For quiet captains gather at my bed
to hear the sagging towers at their backs
kneel down in dust. They have seen hours bleed
in the blue flame of hatred, bleeding wax.
So time that strips the silver from the mirror
breaks our brief sinews; our endeavour breaks,
lying on crumpled blankets, dreaming of terror.

They triumphed for a hand of days: no more:
their outlaw blood burst in the full of the moon.
They walked in purple, warp and pattern of power,
in clash of jewels, lovely stone on stone.
The glance from trembling lashes, lust in a corner,
shot like a pearl between them and the sun;
and all is gone but the dry dust of a banner.

They gather at my bed: they fled the siege,
the burning and the air that ran towards winter;
the rich earth rushing onwards into age
with songs of godhead: to the steady centre
where seasons lay enchained, no weapons rose,
slow daylight crept in circles, and the panther
– the panther-coloured spring – slept in the boughs.

There was Eve's garden, but the fruit was bitter
whose summer practice lured their youth away;
yet quiet roofs were there, and quiet water
suckling the lisping beaches in the bay.
Warm were their cheeks to the warm cheeks of air;
in winglike trees aslant across the clay,
drowsily, birds kept chorus everywhere.

The gnashing axes, and the lightning, fell;
the towers knelt down in dust, hell shook the gardens;
an alien victory thundered in the wheel.

And the world ran like mercury. Their burdens,
borne in concealment, withered up their joy:
the bugles and the honey-breasted maidens,
the time and the attainment, dared not stay.

II

In the unloosed fantastic summer weather
we two alone, my sweeter hemisphere,
sail at evening on the chestnut water.
It's well to see a future without fear:
but you who stare with living lilac eyes
towards that dead east – remember springs, my dear,
and how the soft volcanic light told lies,

and sick endeavour chose the sinister path,
dusk after dusk. And how the horror of birds,
the air with glory spinning like a moth,
the glittering harlequin season, hushed our words.
We had foretold, we thought, the autumnal fox
– and welcomed him, for death was in the cards.
Not this precarious ripeness, when the clocks

have stopped at fifty – and no fifty-one,
leaning to life across the windowsill,
draws back the cinnamon curtains of the sun.
The minutes lick their teeth and mean us ill:
surely from Saracen windows, from this pride
and this aloofness, may our saving skill
not win that older terror which has died?

And you, heart's ease, may still be beautiful,
and all the boats, the hazy spires, the bridges,
no more be stolen, incompatible?
But our need grow the world's need? The wave edges
green as a drake, between the slipping mortar:
oh transient sweet winds, bend your cages!
Towers, neigh out your clamour upon this water!

The river marches to the beat of tides,
unthinking; but the water's riches linger
– the crumpled pool of oars, the haunted reeds,
the crooked willow and the drifting singer
– though drums are in the blood, and something evil,
have taken us by the heart. For these are longer
horizons, beyond sand; the landless level.

For the heart stands on hills; and the high-hung clouds
beat in the mind, follow the sycophant drum.
And love is a pulse that walks our separate bloods,
a clock that ticks in a deserted room:
only a shining sector of the clock,
and puppets gesturing lonely martyrdom
crowd in upon us; wolves that scatter the flock.

Out of precarious conquest, from afar,
relaxing armour, Flodden still to pass,
the captains come, flying the feet of war,
seeing winter grinning secretly through glass.
Their memories are of arcadian earth;
the animal heart, the cat's elastic gaze,
cannot relent before the light of death.

The morning and the Schubert-coloured air,
the mountaineer ambition of the mind,
call us again towards defeat and fear:
the dreamer's door lies open to the wind.
The photographs of summer locked away,
the walls rolled back, the wolves come wailing.
And
the time and the attainment dare not stay.

III

FALLACY ONE FURTHER

Now as I lie, owls in the dark gardens
– swift for destroying, sudden circlers – wail
for no grief; trees have their windy burdens;
and the great idiot moon puts out a sail
for no shore.

So all the postcard hours are folded up,
and wild things inherit us. Oh now,
because I am not listening for your step
in the still, airy room – knowing how
far you are –

I am destroying the night with kindness,
for no joy: while you shiver at the tall
trees that lament, in no greater coldness,
the lesser agony of the hypocrite owl.

IV

What's mine is never separate, but by thousands
– the moment when material flowers in manner:
over our struggle there was no banner
swimming, bright-finned upon a scalene sky;
into our hands
a moment, with the wings of still air,
slid like a bird from thunder secretly:
the lives of worlds were there.

Flame, said the Encheiridion, is a ghost
– Time yet will never think of us at all:
so, Fortune's Lazarus hour-licked, we crawl
towards the accumulated Host.

V

PROTHALAMION

The instant splendour, the swung bells that speak
once to the unprepared glory of youth;
   then the bewildering care:
and nothing more but the stag's backward look,
and the approach of all we were.

And this is the key of the kingdom. Oh my love,
there was a time when the blue-feathered sky,
   the gilded haughty trees,
clad the sardonic rook in the voice of the dove;
when homeward streets were palaces,

and earth was the delight held in a child's hand.
We shook the door, stretched our hands out to the key;
   years closed behind. And yet
we shall not lose that age; it is the hound;
we turn and hear his steady feet.

Over our human purpose winds go
round the unpeopled spaces of the night;
   this night, when we shall join
under their swaying canopy, we know
our heart shall be a child's again.

For they have blown, and the blind stag has fled,
through our perfecting years. The kingdom comes
  though by a narrow gate.
To snare his antlers in his native wood,
the stag runs gladly, soon or late.

This love shall fill the sky again with wings,
and the trees' proud enamel of sunlight be
  as when our eyes were gods'.
Here is the ghostly glory, and the bell swings
here, in the mingling of our bloods.

1935

VI

The word is all: the bell and the wind-bird
clamour and sway so high, the hunted climber
dreams his voice, the lonely moss, his limbs,
are haters in darkness and the dirk in the heather.

The form is nothing: wrath in the unreal storm
eats but the air, terrifies with lights;
ghosts but menace; man soon forgets
the falling of the tower, and the tree-felling.

The only answer lances towards the unknown:
fear in the eyes, the wisdom of a seer
forcing true gods through imagined sources;
hell, in the dreaming heart, heard in the bell.

1939

VII

Clever in rooms, or laughing across fields,
or subtle in the dark by naked windows,
we leave the future in its silken folds,
and wear familiar things; a child's
wonder at purple, at his parents' gold.

Why should that end, inevitable once,
check at love's loneliness? or we though silent
keep the horror out – the mother of stones
upon the tongue, and eyelids of bronze?

These already are watchers in our wood:
dumb as the fate we spell, all understood,
the golden mirror cannot say a word.

1939

VIII

THE INTROSPECTIVE

They rode ahead of death on the strong turning
clocks; and from what cunning
cathedrals of the mind, pure paladins,
they drove the crying dragon. And thence
grew passionless as legends are: for them
Love had, in love, his own Jerusalem.

So victory brought home celestial
thorns, and the rosy grail;
and the long tombs lay down.
Time our tame spider

webs the white hands of the crusader;
misery with fierce eyes prowls his bed
– the cat that eats the faces of the dead.

IX

Salt waters wash the oval fish, and flash
in steamer's wake a week from your lover's look;
the smoky cape and the sea's deep stirring keep
active the ecstasy, open the lack.

Now the old world, the wold, and all you willed,
the merchants, marchers, and the veiled searchers,
are the regrets of sunsets, crumbling sites
leased to the lost dog and the lists of teachers.

In curving scope of scooped waves, towards escape,
such lonely men take meaning for a moon;
under the pale mast sailing they shall feel
the sun and the unseen – and oh how soon!

X

THE SINGERS

I heard them singing in the shadow of sand
how years grow brittle as bread between our fingers,
and the immeasurable miles our garland.
They spoke to the lute with their five-tongued hands,
and I believed the singers.

First March ran over the lawns in gold and silver;
and the wheel shook, and it was May; then
every hour danced on a dulcimer
in citadels of air. After summer
came the thunder of wrath of men,

and days were poison into a clear glass,
coiling from the sky; love was power and terror.
And the heart knew them, tightened like a windlass,
dredging the horrible from unseen places
behind cloaks and mirrors.

Bent as a face watched in a water-bubble,
the sick year stood round us wearing ghosts;
the ghosts called our thought in the voice of the bell:
could we remember March and not tremble?
the singers, undistressed?

I hear them singing, now in flame's shadow,
singing oh lies, lies: now they say
all is forgotten, was very long ago,
the garland was bright ashes, the bread mildew;
and all, faded away.

XI

The man of blood, whose eyes are asphodels,
knows, in the flood of earth, neither remorse
nor exultation. He is drowned in hills;
the widow's hands are warming at his hearse.
His, living, are raised like a star of bone
towards life; and the skull prays between them,

whose paean, sung on tombs, tells the deception
of symbols, blood to engender, flesh to paint;
the bright ship of power, riding corruption.
The man takes nothing; moments are imminent
as water, and the embattled instant is
the branch of olive – the bird that flies back.

XII

IN THE SNOW

My forehead wears the ridge of the world's helmet;
white locusts perch upon my shoulder, and whisper.
I will not hear what the white locusts tell me:
some village plot, Jemima with Sir Jasper,
the drinking and the lecherous hail-fellows,
the poet Alexander and the strumpet,
the virtuous bumpkin, ruddy and triumphant.
And back of all, the gallows.

My newer cap is kinder to the skin.
I doff it humbly, and they let me in
to overheated rooms, the record grinding,
tin-whistle wits contending.
The locusts crowd and scurry upon the panes;
they cannot understand us: we are clever.

The plot is altered, the audience remains.
They sigh a little, and give us up for ever.

XIII

ADAM

He split upon the seamless box of silver
impotent hands; thrust in his father's face
the silence of the glittering revolver;
dragged wounded limbs along a narrow place
between two horrors: till he saw the dream
pursuer, on the naked side of him.

The hair and the dark blood, the sidelong looks,
the tingling of pursuit, the dead weapon,
lay behind. Before, meaningless rocks
rose sharply, empty; and he felt them ripen
like things growing. His long desire was there,
the buried flute that whistled him to her.

He felt a father's teeth upon his throat;
the chisel broke on the dividing wall;
the fountain's blade was crumpled. Then remote
as a bird's cry, daylight; the wonderful
escape, the tunnel pierced. But in his side
death's pain, and a pulsing spring of blood.

XIV

FOUR NOCTURNALS

I

He came by night, offering me
flowers whose throats were clear and red:
turning the door with a dog's knee,
"Sir, buy my wolves," he said.

The yellow and the scarlet wine,
the bare table, the white bread,
he saw: laying his hand on mine,
"Give me this house," he said.

He watched with his etruscan eyes
the quiet phantom on my bed:
flashed in his hand the lifted glass;
"Sweet quicksilver," he said.

II

Whether awake in the dumb night
or losing agony to the sun,
we hear the mocking-bird alight
and speak of things we have not done.
  Makers of music, snap your strings;
  the echoes answer only kings.

Whether alone with burning thigh
or coupled in the reins of fear,
we flinch; the torches die;
and the mocking-bird is near.
  Carvers of beauty, leave your blocks;
  the chisel breaks upon the rocks.

Whether desire in bitterness
or sleeping prophecy of gold,
the robes are torn, the masks eyeless;
and he speaks, and we are cold.
  Coiners of colour, stain your cheeks;
  the mocking-bird is blind, and speaks.

Whether by flame in the sour blood
or green of gyves upon the flesh,
we have listened, we have stood
like broken beasts in a mesh.
        Weavers of words, be dumb, be dumb;
        the night is dangerous, and will come.

III

Now the night lays ghostly charms
in the lover's anxious arms,
and his hapless dreams devise
whispering, the familiar lies
as the futile and the great
go their ways by the same gate.

Formless hands and shadowless
mock us in our meek distress;
one by one nostalgic feet
tread the lonely rainy street;
images of easy tears
follow the false comforters.

Now the trains run roaring through
a hollow sky from me to you,
and destructive resonant things
cross the moon on rigid wings:
but the bridge is broken down
and the homeward signal gone.

Arms outstretched across the bay
lift the lovely hill of day,
but the lover's arms are spread
vainly in his haunted bed.
Time puts out a hand to break
the hearts of them that dare not wake.

IV

The nights are long; and in our wood
  the wakeful satyrs cry:
the horrors of our flesh and blood
  are of infinity.
For still we hear about our bed
the brazen hammers of the dead.

And that which hung enormous dark
  around us, and a gulf
wherein proleptic evils walk,
  and the raging wolf,
turns to his own, and spares no more
the coward thing behind the door.

Softly the living nightmare comes
  and the dead rise, the false,
moving before us to their drums;
  and the deceived heart feels
the clutch of other love; our eyes,
the sorrow of unfaithfulness.

XV

METROPOLIS

...London bridge is broken down...

Pausing with candles upon iron stairs
we think across the river: all you need you purchase
– the electric heavens of omnicompetent stores,
the gilded lifts and public foyers full of torches,
          and the ravishing
          veneer-furnishing.

There your hypnotic children choose the bowler,
muting the gabriel of the blood; there the child's
laurels are belted with marble; the Saturday foot-baller
comes Lazarus from ledgers; shopsoiled ambition builds
  up a mastery
  final as yesterday.

Here the clergyman to Chinese alleys
descends and slums, with flashing teeth; promises
a Mayfair full of minstrel-boys with fat white bellies;
turns our brain-bowery green, would make rickety us
  oh so muscular,
  clean and masculine.

A penny tram returns him to the edges,
the suburbs of minds, to see the houses like
a pile of tickets; or to dreamers' villages
within the Underground, where only pigeons look
  at the eternal
  War-memorial.

Chase if you will his happy car, that threads
the almond lawns, the prettiest of postal districts;
here's the hot cellar, the arch in the dangerous roads,
where not for beauty or bounty the rodent boy instructs
  rat-sisters, labouring
  into the labyrinth.

These have the sour virtue of being alone,
the ravagers of railings, the secret marauders;
born to no god's metropolis in the sun
of acceptance; gallant walkers, desolate riders
  forth; yet furtively
  active and lovely.

Candled on iron stairs (see now), their hands
raised against rotting metal, shadows of souls.
The streets run homeward (hear now) like the cry of hounds,
to you, in outer light, whose infinity cancels
        with Bank Holiday
        no man's malady:

home from the living centre, westward ho
to death; and the still houses evil as new oceans.
Here's the machine with teeth, here in the gas limbo,
(feel now) the running terror; the wheel's revolutions
        faster, and fatal
        upon the metal.

Where, in what circle of this real hell
(or in the drab not-world your chanting Dante finds
towards green pastures), where is the end – the whole
of hiding or of living? the beast, the core of minds,
        in its ivory
        park of slavery?

Lost. Leave then, in the shadow of pigeons, defiant
children living – to unbuild the city, exploit
the crumbling bridge, fight the invading worm, hold the fiend
fast. And oh to these, though flanked by fear and blindness, let
        from the ambush rise
        tongues, and creative eyes!

XVI

THE ISLANDERS

Crouched in the womb I learned this fear:
the subtle streams that fed me moved
in darkness, and my fish's ear
took dimly from the outer air
nothing I knew or loved.

Then between lifted thighs I broke
into a bed of weeping; found
strong to the pouring air as rock,
and grimly rooted like the oak,
the inevitable round.

A farthing frond of beauty hid
the weevil in my green delight;
but round my pillow came the dead,
and the unborn were garmented
in guttering wicks by night.

Then to that other darkness came
behind my lidded eyes, the blood
that beat me around me in the womb;
under my fingers crept the worm
of bonds and solitude.
Now the great bones of ancient things
lie foundered on the rotting beach;
the fear of death betrays our tongues;
our beds are full of whisperings:
blind, we turn each to each.

We lift involuntary hands
out of our separate dream; but still
the goblin like a gantry stands
with arms forbidding, and unwinds
the fibres of the soul.

Lights wander between us, and we crouch
while inaccessible pain and love
fasten upon the external touch:
silent around us, the worlds watch
our useless fear of death and life.

XVII

AT THE WINDOW

The wind leaps back from brick, in the dark field
the hammers are stilled;
pillowed on living world, the stone stares
breathless, the wanderer counts impossible stars.
But you my spring my builder of beauty,
waking or sleeping across miles of roads,
walk in my labour with immaculate body
and memories of trees and Chinese birds,
as out of dust Lent's windy charity brings
boughs and bright wings.

Five white flames, but cold, I touch upon
this curving pane;
and all my heart is gathered suddenly close
like a cat's pupil, seeing behind the glass
the yellow clock, content: emotional shadow
softens my looking-out upon past years
– the midnight market, all the world a widow

– and this pale beating hand which is not yours.
Your brittle shell of air tames like a dove
the beast of love.

Over that fluid ghost, under the skin,
passion goes on;
back from the triple crossings, and the hours
of long inactiveness, the sleep of towers.
For now when streets are silent, and earth sways
gently in the night's caressing cradle,
keels run awake and easily in curled seas
and sailors dream above the steady needle;
and the dark hands of hills drop to the earth
their violet wreath.

Sail in my silence like the electric swan:
hands on the pane
are trembling, minutes prowl for enemies;
feet are in haunted places, no rockets rise.
Come like the bird, come like the branch-flowered river,
to the unbuilding of our living earth:
out of all oceans morning's neck of silver
bursts and will sing, and part us with her breath.
Then hammers fall, and wings, and one awakes;
and the bough breaks.

XVIII

THE HUNT

Running to you, as the sad beast runs home,
I lock the one door with proleptic dying
– then face the hound. No further terror of him.

Out of the days of my savannah-daring
the wind blows back to you; the final cave
where only, life being so, is death worth doing

and worth withstanding. An hour will carve
these spiral galleries; thought like a rodent
gnaws, into time, patterns as bodies curve.

Little the fox, although the roofs are reddened,
mourns for that image; the drowned recalls
no dolphin; he does not fear the trident:

it is the fact, it is the freedom, kills;
manner of comfort, the closed place of harm,
are you – the core of my tightening circles,

that run to you as the sad beast runs home.

XIX

Time will not open his clenched hand;
there are green shields before the sun;
over the king and the king's hound
the everlasting sand is sown.
Gods that were falcons, and gods horned,
stir in the mighty loin of rock:
time will not open his clenched hand
– their wings dry, their wands break.
So in a brooding night of gold
lie wills unborn, and buried will,
and we – their sole immortal child
(time will not open his clenched hand)
– not dead, but in a life more still,
spent arrows, in desired land.

XX

Lovers have wept and been afraid
because they found all beauty come
down to the biting of the spade
and the falling-back of loam.

But the wild blue-eyed unicorn
rages upon heraldic air;
the brooding eyes within us mourn
there. You are burnt with beauty there.

The legend or the virgin dies;
the trembling beast beside her stands
watching the sun between her thighs
and the white garland of her hands.

Painted or dreamt her life and his,
her death and his, are steady-starred:
they have two immortalities,
the chevron of a sudden bird.

XXI

Choosing evocative words, we lift our hands
towards the five ambitions of men;
and in our night the fireworks gush tomorrows
bringing no fear,
but each a penny Jupiter.
Fingers, creators of our world, knowers
of the heart's lustful cipher, the soul's
script; who feel strange roads through music, furrow
the springing sea:
have you no power to hear, to pray?

You have given us the limpid lovelady
in towers of sunlight, in wooden fields
before a shout of hands; her lacquered eyes
and the blind breath
that haunts the actor: is there no path
where speaking dolls, where fears that come alive,
mock us but cannot reach to us?
Tomorrows are all earth; it is the past
that's terrible.
We had made plans for burial.

In green half-living houses of the dead,
with voices of sack-cloth and glass,
creatures await the mouldering beauty of
the angelus.
Here also resurrection is;
but five ambitions and the art of hands
made crosses and huge wombs of lead:
this was to happen in the dead of winter;
one more season,
there would have been no gate to that prison.

But what we buried was a thing living.
Fingers, creators of our world,
why could you not lay hold of life, as of
invented things?
Choosing evocative words, we hang
our hearts upon the five ambitions of men;
but clasp our knees in Babylon:
oh penta-Danaë, free spirits march
beneath your tower:
the graven mansions' terrible choir.

XXII

ALEXANDER

The cæsar of the world cast his crown
into the heavens' flood,
thinking the fiery spaces watched his toy
and saw it drown.
But the seventh heaven would be God:
the perfect hour looks for infinity:
into a hope beyond their spheres
looked upward, stars.

There is an image in the death of trees:
men creep into their bone;
and the birds sing, because ambitions fail,
in their dead boughs.
Our living is a shell between
the crooked beggar and the nightingale;
and cæsar into circling waves
cast eyes, not leaves.

XXIII

THE SEASHELL

Locked in my shell of bone and blood
  an ocean says diminished things;
the echoes of the lover's head,
  her million mouths and green tongues.

Clasping its coloured horn, you sail
  inward along the fathomless
desired horizon of the shell:
  are voices then the breadth of seas?

Dumb in the prison of distance, that
  which stained this mockery in her gulf
stamps to destroy us: the white feet
  of the dragon, passion herself.

XXIV

In the cruel breasts of grecian statuary,
the oiled bodies of athletes, the arrogant
                awakeners of the flesh,
is Diotima: between flame and us
move the unspeculative masks, are cut
                the adamant friezes.

Plotinus on the waterfront saw souls
lighting the outward unreal mesh of trees
                and rooted hills: saw in
that darkly-sweeping spirit the bastion
of all tangible things, the whirlpool of the blood
                with the unknown.

Perfected forms – the coloured rock, the flower,
or the shot-silk of breasts – in these a soul
                dwells like a minotaur:
the spirit of the spiral, the ghost born
between earth and unattainable fire;
                and resting here.

So, in those sensual imaginings,
those mindless chiselled blocks, there is implied
                (higher than brain or blood)
that thought to which all beautiful belongs:
the ocean air, the godhead and the god
                – artesian things.

The flesh is innocent, the stone is chaste;
but in the absolute and behindward ghost
the power and passion is.
The life of things is cruelty and lust:
girdled, we falter, in the adamant frieze
of entities.

What dreams of porcelain majesty endure
the hands of angels, the soul's shattering bell?
This is the iron hell,
the ineluctable bond of impure
power: if you are living, soul, you, you're
my sensual shell.

XXV

All were lovely, and with vivid souls
fathered their beauty in remorseless things:
in tortured webs of stone, miracles
of breathless craft, the creation of wings.
For some were artificers, flaxen-limbed
and weeping wine from the plumed eyes of angels;
some had eagles' hearts, and were ashamed
of human languor, limbs not like an eagle's.
They were a golden catching of the breath;
silken light moved round them as they walked.
They were all axle-bearers, the wheel
a sunflower, a turning of the earth.
They were all spirits of an hour, an act,
shining in the masks you made beautiful.

XXVI

Than lifeless rock, then, the racked heart no more
feels in itself, being loveless: dead objective
things, born to no knowledge; wings hewn but never active.
So do insentient springs coil outwards; mere
fact that stands by witness – the whiteness of
hands; or the heart that knew not it lacked love.

Self is a function: so the sylph in stone,
spiritless, yet had perfection – dumb
because thoughtless – that no thought became.
And so your beauty was Pygmalion:
for when you gave me being, why afterwards
give this desire that soars but has no words?

XXVII

Consider, metaphysical my heart,
the blood of birth and dying: when between
dark hemispheres, that cannot soothe or hurt
the crying flesh, lie virgin or outworn
two immortalities composed in one.

Our fathers' passion, fearing the power that lay
in stones or the green lion of the trees,
turns through our lips; and there the unborn lie
and the forgotten beast within us roars
to his mate, tramples tomorrow's rose.

You then my love, time's and blood's islander
– because we fear the unicorn – lie down
as powerless as they. For the tides dare,
the tides do, all that our dreams have done:
endless perfection, heart, locked and curved in.

XXVIII

The grecian tulip and the gothic rose
flower to deceive us; limbs age with fruits;
the man who marks the boneyard with a cross
reaps poppies; human flesh plucks down the roots
of the barley. The greyhound with the kind
sensitive head and the soft eyes, goes blind
or mad; dies. The wind means all it cries.
Love, it is time we listened to that wind.

Who cranes an arm to wait for the white body,
death, polishing old philosophies,
gives the grave scarves woven of our beauty.
Beasts are passive as growing rings of trees;
perfected process lacking hope or thought,
tulip-limbs, or the white rose in the throat.
To die as those die, live as the lion knows
– love, it is time we found that secret out.

XXIX

THE LIONS

Mute in the arc-light stands
time with a whip; their loins
cringe, on blunted paws. His hands
are twisted in their manes.
They circle at his commands.

Meek and magnificent
from cages, the gelded lions
fawn on our intent,
fearing punishment.

They rushing in darkness were
eyed like the sun with rage;
living sulphur, a fire.
But love stripped Samson's hair.
We beat them to our cage.

XXX

TRANSMUTATION

Out of the air, the metal wings of gulls
the clever harriers, the scream and flash;
out of the cradle, the desires of girls,
the folded garments, hands upon the flesh.
Out of the ape, the dreams of strangers – fear;
out of the childless, the enchanting tongue;
fire from the echoing earth, from ether fire;
this moment, this design, from everything.

Not manner, then, but medium – time, not form
– is the external motion: we have been
the salamander in the iron flame,
the symbol, and the carving upon bone.
We shall have been the enmity, the feeling
of death; and one by one the planets falling.

XXXI

EPITHALAMION

Wind in the street, and sadness of unknown walkers
in a world shut-out; infinite sadness of men
not, this night, one and quiet with my love:
look down, stars, you illimitable and glorious wakers,
on her delight that wakes from silks; her, the young moon,
her bright body stepping to me, perfect, unaloof,
                    moving in life;
rising with no shame, towards Endymion.

Oh swift lights that sweep through your proud abysses,
and stretch your power along the infinitesimal days of man,
this shall escape you, this you shall not dissolve.
Have we not checked you, winging wind, stars in your courses,
bound you in a twilight of all times, made our demesne
in the still courts of the chimera, silenced moment and self?
                    Together, the gulf
walled-in, body and life made one?

Life in life, spirit in spirit, as the earth moves
for ever gently in the swaying of night's harness,
one peace; as now earth rests, and all the
ships have untroubled ways in their white grooves,
and waters go among them on caressing journeys;
and our imprisoned prophecy steals wide and free
                    as the pouring pools of the sea,
strong indissoluble wonder of deep clearness?

No future, no fear now, in this hushed house stirring;
only our breaths bound, linked the circle of our years,
and the past rising present against sleep.
I have taken the world in a small room, oh high staring
night, our flesh made perfect; mine to be ours.

And the strong promise lays its head upon my lap:
                    him will I keep,
here in the burning of our mutual fires.

And the fires burn down; faces return from glass;
we are not waking, dead, sleeping: we are still,
in timelessness, the flower shaken from the bough.
And shadows move in the deep breath of weariness;
in peace, unknowing, endeavour turns to the wall.
And the wheel's quietness is promise. Now
                    we murmuring only know
the immemorial splendour of the wheel.

XXXII

Here on the windy balcony
we face together, you and I
the desert of the apogee:
clasp cold hands, begin to see
the future and its final sky.

There will be some who see it all
as distant glory; drum to war
those who will even fight and fall
in the ecstasy of the animal.
We know what we are fighting for,

whose monstrous teeth are at our throat
bloody and brilliant and stark;
and why we shall not shut him out
at last, or hope to go about
and fish for comforts in the dark.

The world is weary of harness now,
the open, the tumultuous:
shutter the window, let the bough
be plucked that blossoms God knows how.
The smell of death is over us.

Hope will break the windlass, and
achievement slip the rising mesh:
sit still, count your contraband
– the cloths of night, the imploring hand,
the secret shuttle weaving flesh.

XXXIII

NEGOTIUM PERAMBULANS IN TENEBRIS (PSALMS 91:5)

Evil has walked whispering in our curtains
and crept into our beds; we have understood
the pulsing eyes of cats, their soft motions,
and the inhuman thumbprint grained in wood.
These have possessed us, haunted our escapes
from frozen dreams, the quietness of gardens,
and immemorial stones in angry shapes.
Evil has walked at noonday in our curtains,
melting the muscle, never darkening
the populous window; steaming from the earth
unseen as air is, tangible as heat.
We have observed in the air, flying feet;
turned from our lives to hear the satyr sing;
hated, and seen the idol hold its breath.

XXXIV

Towards, my love, those disappearing hills
whose clouds are combative: for there
swan-feathered ladies are
in crying water and the sway of gulls.
The ways of death are hooked and steep;
here the Egyptian mothers weep
to see winged Herods in their sleep:
but we must climb the waterfalls
towards those disappearing hills.

Forget, my love, those shining spiders'-coils;
quiet the swift worm of the blood:
hard are the runner and the road,
the terrible jointed height where lightning falls.
The black dog in the thunderstone
strips the flesh from star and moon
with teeth fast in living bone:
but a blue-handed beacon calls
towards those disappearing hills.

Forget your English roofs and watery meadows;
and streets wherein the tears of Blake
blossom out of stones, and speak;
and the cold arms clutching from the shadows:
though our separate hearts must climb
moving-downward-stairs of time,
we have been arrows in a dream
of disappearing mountains where
the swan-feathered ladies are.

XXXV

EGYPT 1940

I

Now the night finds us; the bright worlds advance
leaning across Europe's planted lines
to the uncertain sea
and the Americas.
            The night finds us the body betrays us
            and love devours us and time passes.

This is the hour when carnival is over
and colours drain from things; the fallacy
of patient landscapes darkening,
and man's habitation.
            The body betrays us and love devours us
            and time passes and none saves us.

Now the room empties and the walls are down;
the selves of us are naked in the gulf,
stripped of interval
and place and circumstance.
            Love devours us and time passes
            and none saves us and strength fails us.

Neither our flesh nor that which inwardly
watches, be separate now: alone that touch
is proof against the close
and final need of death.
            For time passes and none saves us
            and strength fails us and wideness withers.

And all our thought has grown the house of war:
the resting senses await him; friendly things
look strange, and soothe no longer

our rebellious lust.
          For none saves us and strength fails us
          and wideness withers and earth forsakes us.

Still the cold bed of being two, the sharp
and screaming rack of Europe, must for all
our metaphysics, all
our living, be; and last.
          Strength fails us and wideness withers
          and earth forsakes us.
                              And night finds us.

II

Who are they, the impending wanderers
between the shadow and the wall between
desire and the will's apprehension?
A watchfulness in the eyes' corner?
Rapunzel falls our evening; and our tears
fall, from the unreal to the unseen,
and still the watchers from the hems of death
(unhailed echoes, dissolving fingers) paint
hope's wide eyes upon a windy cloth:
weaving two pennons, two desolations,
the floating hair of distance, and the fins
of war. And wanderers devilish in our blood.

And they have blood of tears. Oh stand upon
this eminence of mourning night, look down
over your carpet of arcadian earth,
till that unreal glory dies
in our life, and the invisible remains
– an everlasting darkness and a dream.

Oh but the haunters in our sunless ways.
Not the mercurial anger of iron, flare

of the flying poison, oblique lashes;
but the internal apparition:
the pox of crooked motions, calloused
endurance; shrouded fittings of disease.

It is the sweet beleaguered past makes mad,
bends the straight-falling shadow, corrupts
the body's bravery and grace, and
the trained machinery of living:
till mirrors crane from an abandoned room,
those are eyes which round a throat were pearls,

and the imagined dead branch like a coral.
Sea-drunken men with bayonets have burst
from the ineffectual guardroom
of history; weeping triumph dozes
upon the red-sea wreck; a pirate night
shakes out her colours.
Deluge begins.

III

Who shall discover our last eminence?
The mind is made like Andalusian towers,
rings, like a tree with age,
the cores' Atlantic stone.
Uncertain ocean waves the weathercocks
when all's over, the parent punished;

but we stand masked upon the inland piers
of a new world, in time of nightingales.
This finally: for now
is the uproaring end,
with wisdom changing and selves wasting
abyss of beauty and fear within us.

For love's the dweller by our Acheron,
the Fury in the bird among the tombs:
whose loud desolate singing
has betrayed us to
the beast with fingers in the shadowy hall
tapping our shoulder as time passes.

Too easily, my dear, we have rebelled
for this intangible embrace, which comes
to plots and weeping in
the enemy night. This will not
save the colour of our eyes; but only
                    that time passes and love devours us.

Nor will our minds discover how to wear
incurious armour blindly to endure
the crystal hands that move
with unrelenting power
                    the living and the dead. For time passes
                    and love devours us. The body betrays us.

Rest. With usurping steps, bright worlds advance
Juno's curved wing, leaning their savage eyes
to the Americas
and legendary day.
                    Time passes and love devours us
                    the body betrays us.
                                        And night finds us.

THE COLLECTED POEMS

THE INWARD ANIMAL

(1943)

FOREWORD

The first and the last of these poems present (in a social and a religious mode respectively) the pattern of a personal experience that must now have been shared by many. The rest of the book is my own mode of this experience. Now that the war has taken millions from their familiar environment and associates, its impact and the impact of strangeness must have shaken, and perhaps destroyed, many a customary self. There will have been a shocked and defensive rebellion; reconciliation must follow; the birth of some mutual thing in which the old and the new, the self and the alien, are combined after war. This childbirth is not easy; the pain is sure to be there.

For myself, and for many in the same or a worse position, I have tried to express the three parts of this pattern: the first distress; rebellion against place and circumstance; slow mutual absorption ending in the birth of something at once myself and a new self and Egypt. The "inward animal" is this child, so unwillingly conceived and carried, so hardly brought forth.

TERENCE TILLER
CAIRO 1942-3.

I

ECLOGUE FOR A DYING HOUSE

1. This was the county; all was firm here; nothing
deciduous – not the trees, the weeping pines
and holms, the discreet mourning of the yews.
The spreading houses had a hundred roots
in narrow blood the very bricks blushed firm with
and did not tell the seasons: centuries nest there.
The lawns like an escutcheon, the suave gardens
quiet, yet burning with memorial flowers;
and the stone wyverns at the gate set fast
in gentlemanly consciousness of worth.
2. Beyond is the gnarled land, fertile and fierce
and scarred with pregnancies; the armpit land
of old unshaven things. And here all is
earthy and sweaty. Or ethereal England
hesitant in the hawthorn or the lake:
the melancholy sweetness and the bitter
struggle,
3. labour and harvest and death,
2. the stones
impregnable as leaves; the growing earth
and all its guardians,
3. plougher and sower and parson,
2. born to be weary, not blind to beauty. Beyond,
the busy towns, queer friendly villages;
salt streets of ports, and the unbiddable sea.
1. But
here was the county, broadly built on squires,
the hunting owners bred in bone, the very
rich.
2. In what?
1. They were inheritors.
2. Of what?

3. Of all they were not and that lived
 cruelly for them: peasant soil, pangs
 of the soil, effortless earth in flower
 upon the dead and broken, the great breast
 pouring riches to their mouths.
2. They gave?
1. They gave like virgin land, accomplishment
 of self; security in self; unlaboured plenty
 growing and seeding as itself; and were not
 virgin. Like a freed wilderness, but were pathed,
 plotted, were bred or might not breed; like nature
 and were man's mosaic. Time – but their own excuse.
2. No more?
1. A green December; immortal bone.
2. Bone does not live, bone does not bear.
3. Bone rots.
2. Perennials blow down; bricks crumble.
3. The bone rots.
 The daddy-long-legs and the mole destroy.
2. Fertility feeds on stone.
3. And the bone rots.
2. All the dear delicacy and the power,
 the artificial swan upon the river,
 the winged imperial fish aloof in marble,
3. the gallant gardens and the herald's cold
 impossible domain,
2. all the unique
 unfertile chosen things –
1. – their own excuse –
2. – things chosen by birth for birth
3. – birth brings them down.
2. The delver and the reaper stay.
3. Earth does
 not blow away.
2. Mud mothers.
1. You are speaking

the old inconsequent sermon of mortality,
the parable of Adonis; or are pastoral
fools, gilding the sordid mattock: *Mother*
Earth; Dame Nature; honest, honest ploughman;
oh happy shepherd.
2. We do not speak of these,
the tired lessons of decay and growth,
or the romantic with white hands commending
an unreal pastoral envy. Not of these
individual things, of your own prizes, not
of a creed; but symbols.
3. And of things
that are; of double things. A different truth.
1. What of my faith, these living monuments?
3. That do not live.
1. The House; things as they are?
2. They are not. These are glamour upon spires;
the last reel running from the light, leaving
shadows; a canvas pillar in a masque:
fine within fiction, memorable, habitual.
But not to live by.
1. To preserve.
2. You cannot.
3. The bone rots.
2. These were never bone, but garments
of proud walkers.
3. These the moth or the horned
hand steals from glory, and the naked rise
clothed in the shaggy earth, limbs of the earth.
2. Daughters and sons, the country garden and
the heath; the rowan or elm; the wavering fenland
or the crag. The matron land that swells to
human fathering.
3. And the beauty that
is only beauty.
2. And the men that die

as generations, never as man.
1. But these,
the county, have not died.
3. And yet the House
is full of death; years and lives are its dust,
thick on the cornice, the great staircase, on
the supercilious heads and horns and masks,
the quarterings that died as generations:
it is past labour, beauty, ignorance,
2. cruelty and calm,
3. love and enforced love,
2. war
from whose anguish birth and death together
rose to a twilight and were death again;
3. the ghost of gowns, the odour of a thousand
dancing feasts: the House is full of death.
All the unseeing windows speak it; all
the fountains pouring blindly to the cold;
here is an attic of dead toys: dead time
powerful in the smallest mote or leaf,
but not alive.
2. Active, but not alive.
3. It is a cloud of spirits in the House:
2. death and the time that is death.
3. The dying House
waits like a beast for a new life to eat,
or like a shell, for a new inmate. Human
selfhood against time, its symbol.
2. Down
by the garden tank, by the proud laurels, is
running water from a world not part
of its world. Here the life is thin and small
but stirring, while the untended gardens run
back to the outer soil and seed, and insect
war enlaces war of plants. The rooms
hollow and servantless, sink deep into

their own decay and brooding, madmen that glower
into themselves in darkness, animals'
leaping-inward fury; without thought,
but hating; without life, but dangerous.
3. Still the pool stirs with life, the common river
bleeds to it. Life is overthrowing you:
the water murmurs in your cellars.
2. Water
is in your walls.
3. And the dry cistern threatens
after rain.
1. Let nothing come. This is
my county: honour its dust the spider watches.
Leave the triumphant mouse his play. My flesh
dries on the bone –
3. Bone rots
1. – and will not rise.
Will not accept. Will thrust out the strange seed.
2. You may desire, or will may be accomplished
– will, but not your will always. For a time
the struggle and the individual pain,
victories over will.
3. And for a time
the will that is not willed; house-echoes, or
the rush of gravity;
2. power that cannot withhold
power; self-memory sleeping whipped by darkness
to spin, totter and fall, and the earth not shake.
And then the birth, fathered by strangers,
3. full
of the water and the laurel,
2. full of the cries
of birth, and the child riding blood; and full
of alteration out of agony.
Down by the garden tank, the laurel-bearing
lawn, he is standing, hearing the common river.

There, he is thoughtful as a conqueror;
the time of change.
1. Dust that has come to dust,
and will be dust. We are unconquerable.
2. Release the time of change, set free the action;
we cannot hold or help.
1. I can destroy.
2. None can destroy. We cannot help or hold.

II

THE PARDONER'S TALE

And on the ground, which is my moodre's gate,
I knokke with my staf, bothe erly and late.
And seye, "Leeve mooder, leet me in!
Lo how I vanysshe, flesh and blood, and skyn…"
Chaucer, The Pardoner's Tale, 729–32

I

Since the bare bone, and since
the glistening sinew, press
naked together, wince
at mutual nakedness
– for flesh and skin but gloss
the rails they're stretched across:

men must conceal their love
with glamour about the bone,
prank and patch and glove
that sensual skeleton,
till only their desires,
and not themselves, are liars.

II

So the desire that cannot live
is given features and a voice;
that echo from the limbs of love
answers anarchy with vice
– an outward ecstasy compressed
in the unwilling masochist.

Then what remains to lose or vaunt
– beauty, wit, or words of skill?
What angel amnesties prevent
the scraping death around the skull?
– then what creation stripped of fear
hungering turns conqueror?

III

So I was driven forth
out of my discontent:
by narrow paths I went
homewards and into death.

I journeyed night and day,
sunrise to moon's set;
but never once I met
a fellow on the way.

Till at my mother's gate
I paused, and heard the mouse
cry kingship of the house
– and knew I was too late.

III

BIRTHDAY POEM

The fingers close upon the hour,
slow scissors: hold them back:
there is a mirror in the clock
as candid as a schoolmaster.

The spider in the hour-glass
knows when to net her soft eclipse
upon the double Mars of lips,
and ebb with ripples round your face.

Time has overdrawn your bank
of comeliness: Elizabeth
looked in the silver and saw death:
you are older than you think.

The tendrils of delight, as wicks
are shrivelled, struggle to creep in
to the stems where they were born;
illusion smoulders back to sex.

Is there another topic? None:
it is the symbol of the sword;
time like an ace, the gunners' card;
war like a radio sealed on.

Man who gave them and gave you life
in blind ecstasy must behold
each bitter wasted envious child
ignobly dying of itself.

Clocks have a will to execute:
you are left a space to live
by the snapping tomb; you have
inherited the worm and rat.

Another curling of this thumb,
a nearer crouch of stalking blades;
death's a full house; be sure, he bids,
your birthday is a trick to time.

So if I greet you now, I can
but wish you older when you die
not of the outer enmity
but the uncivil war of man.

IV

The silence that I break was more profound,
and purer, sound
– as being absent is a kind
of closer bridal, in the mind.
Nor do my words create
the peace they imitate.

Again I spoil with them the gentle thought
silence had brought,
painting that inward armistice
with child's, but unperspective, eyes;
in the real kiss knew yet
unions more close than it.

No threatenings then of temporal campaign
shall steal again
our spoken silence and our speech

that needs no silence each to each;
not space nor presence mar
the better thing we are.

V

The lines that mathematics draw
(angular circumscription of
the curved impatience of a paw;
the eccentric swell of love)
define but cannot rule at all
the leaping inward animal.

The leaping inward animal
(the satyr in his lonely wood,
the lamb in his Wordsworthian dale)
makes every leap a maidenhead;
nor can the printed place foresee
where next those lusty feet may lie.

Where next those lusty feet may lie
(in pitfalls for the grinning wolf
or by the writhing iron sea)
is a great sickness in itself
whose large enfevered motions flaw
the lines that mathematics draw.

VI

THE INWARD ANIMAL

Grief is not you, nor are
the form and inward form
of you the thin despair
that whispers of your harm.
Still there are ways that leave
no valiance at all,
not of the mind but of
the inward animal:

that which is lustful in
the selves' enchanted bond,
or sees a robber when
hand is on trusting hand;
that which is death when else
I am a fire of peace,
pours tides across my pulse,
negations in my face;

the primitive revolt
against a mind or will,
the blood of Abel spilt
in cups already full.
Being and feeling and thought
are but a naked man
who fights what he is not,
the animal within.

We are their fields; their path
the peace of me-and-you;
their long discourteous wrath
the civil war of woe.
Knowledge and now conflict;

nor have I power enough
only to live your fact
and the name of grief.

VII

THE BLIZZARD IN THE BOTTLE

Sometimes in the cages of night, in work
that is not of the heart,
as once in another year, another dark,
she is there across the room, reading; gilt
by a common lamp, tired by a common end,
that part us though they join: so she would go,
and be tonight tomorrow's contradiction.

Our love appeared to us in little
gestures, in words; and yet
our lonely rooms knew granite, knew the battle,
knew the air, of love that was not spilt
over apparent lips but lay profound
in a drift of images, immediate though
denied the link and lamplight of an action.

The blizzard in the bottle, weather
captured yet remote,
unreal unless the eye itself can gather
perspectives to a pupil: so I have felt
her, in space and history, though beyond
their glass – as if at the war's end that ends too,
or to be separate were our imperfection.

Now I scramble at the wire
of a tall Present, but
the old immediacy of love is there
as once in a former country when we built
in common work and sentience, the land
of equal things: gentle as air, but true
and necessary as the world's direction.

VIII

The oracle's desire for darkness gave
the inward window and the empty dome:
you being gone, I plot a concave
world, a sky-camera, where no light may come.

I cannot grow into the sun-flower,
as the insensitive garden turns towards light,
the summer-cock; your image, and none newer,
lies on this unstarred chamber's silvered plate.

The world gives back, upon the veiled tripod,
the single answer whose syllables reflect
immovably the presence of a god
hidden by the recording architect.

IX

EXAMINATION ROOM

Gazing from wistful eyes across bowed heads
I think the lost romantic lover's thought
of when there fluttered in my net
fire-singing-birds,
and I also sang in cords
being content with slavery; of what
in agony has by the iron floods
befallen. And precipitate longing stirs,
among these endless writers, into tears.

Useless indeed the arrow's backward gaze
and the string broken; the confederate past
stares like a prison from a waste
where I like these
willed excessive masteries,
creating metaphors. Time now has cost
a million words, spirits or animal lies;
and they have bought no future, but this less
oh less than strength, this concave watchfulness.

I am to guide these futures, to approve
their common copying of certain steps;
who have pulled ribbons from my lips
for them, for love,
coloured with myself – conjuring life
– and been the Merlin of soaring hopes.
Who now am sitting with them, writing of
the spirit-patterns of the necromancer
till the bell rings on the unfinished answer.

GIZA.

X

The acid of the heart bleaches my morning.
The cleverness of lust grows commonplace.
Thought is intangible and has no meaning.
One who came gently with a winter's grace
into the fire of passionate concealing
turns with remoteness to a shrouded face,
the body a bandage over feeling:
the limb torn off, its agony remaining.
All endures, the waiting the defiling.
Thought is intangible and has no meaning.

Now all our minutes dream of aftermaths,
and the returning dust becomes a symbol.
We lie alone dying incessant deaths
but it is not for dying that we tremble:
here at a touch the lemon-painted flax
the jewelled mummy of our years may crumble;
Marvell's chariot thunders at our backs;
time passes time, the dream seductions pass,
into this wind of blood this wandering sex.
The cleverness of lust grows commonplace.

I the endurer am the mocker of me.
One who was music is a silent house:
under the hammers of this iron sea
the light arms of love turn tremulous
and there is no assurance between kisses.
Oh it is all uncertainty of choice
as the achievement or the humour passes
– thought being intangible, having no meaning
– as after dreams of horrors or embraces
the acid of the heart bleaches my morning.

XI

Being oneself: the last and worst exclusion,
unit's enclosure of communal nothing.
        There is a prison,
or a deserted village, in my breathing:
        where is your strength, soft bitter *one*,
        to hurl stones at another stone,
breaking its windows? or to break your own?

Setting of action: the falling blood
in the picture; or the behind-a-pictures inns
        to which all roads lead:
flowing and fighting through a million loins
        I am born a coloured stone
        to hurl bones at another bone
under the barren claw of a closed moon.

XII

ELEGY I

Cairo 1941

Here in the slouching gloom, dusky with nooses,
horror the rat-catcher parades
this mockery of fecund glades,
threading the whistling laughs and flagrant kisses,
the awkward nightlife of the running company:
the miserable rat-catcher, the ghost
of what is given or lost;
the stalking menace of the castaway.

Four elements, black angels, walk this ground;
no god; no beckoning halo roams
these empty cold and captive tombs
arid as rock, as the split bone beyond;
four elements and their possessing Moloch, battle
of blind or innocent, the wasting fire
whose murderous embers bar
the hopeless turning in the ring of metal.

But here there is the shadow of the ring,
motes of darkness that will blind
our senses, have our pity chained;
cadaverous falcons that on sterile wing
stoop to the glamour and gaudiness and seize apart
the broken light; brown carrion of horror,
the sidling nightmare surer
than love, corrupting life, or the stabbed heart.

Deciduous almanacs snow out the year,
and a cathedral chill is cast
over despair and thought and lust:
hell in the aisles and in the belfry fear.
The uncertain daffodil of our inordinate pity
may never bloom again; the earth is spread
rusty and heavy with dead
past hearing, past spring's instigating beauty.

Now only blood and a black wind; and cold
that is not of clean growing things
– March in the moorland's planted wings,
or unleashed muscle in the dancing field.
Oh it is death's invasion of no innocence,
the crumbling fall of Now. Our chartless soul
wasting about the Pole,
the city of love's bruised magnificence.

XIII

DESERT

Moses' feathery devils out of sand
sway melting westward: bleak old-virgin land
dreaming of children – tree, and hearth, and jet
of the tame shadowed fountain – casts them out
like a nun's dream of man. They will be sown
a terrible abstinence upon limbs of stone,
the red infertile trunks and rocky thighs
absorbing their own seed.
                                        What lands are these?
Not Adam's earth; nor is this wind the fire
of breath creating gratified desire.

Still where the viper swims in sand, the pearly
scorpion stiffens, and the flat-mouthed surly
lizards are – here, looking towards the waste,
we know more bare an impotence than dust
or the dry ant-clean spectres that are born
of it, or venom of the scale and horn.

Over my bed there fumes a scented stick
– the circumcision of the catholic
– to me an image of this desert, poured
in sterile fire to cense a fruitless lord.
It grew of Adam's earth, a race that fell:
the sick and fleshy richness of the Nile.

TEL-EL-KEBIR.

XIV

EGYPTIAN RESTAURANT

Now I have dropped a stone in the reflection,
broken the room into a thousand rooms:
a thousand edges of acute refraction
blaze in the mirrors, in whose toss of beams

we sit as under a spray of images,
real where all is fleeting, plural, like
the circling crowd of jewelled ghostly Us.
Here is a stir, a glare, to crush the weak!

– rustle and babble and clang, fearful illusion
of lights and odours, doubling and gone and again,
where the soft-footed waiters tread precision
to terror's edge, and yet are voiced like men.

Crossing and re-crossing, the dark faces,
earth under flower-pots, wetly gape and gleam;
are lost in brightness, fall in tiny pieces,
move in and out of an appalling womb

as food is built and broken. Among these
one, who can clutch with bitterness the last
infirmity, the knowledge that he is:
he droops his shoulders like the fading rest,

stares down the room where it is always raining
– lost in a mist of mirrors as in tears,
cloth over arm, silver and glassware shining
– a mournful waiter among the chandeliers.

RESTAURANT EL HATI, CAIRO.

XV

STREET SCENE

Down glittering rows the windows run
displaying you in shoes or books,
your silk and linen draped upon
a thousand simpering yous in wax.

And all the owners' peering hopes
and the assorted crowds that pause
or stare unseeing at the shops,
are you before a looking-glass.

Marking his makers' thrust about,
the statue in the square maintains
through whatsoever change of light
a high authoritative stance.

The passing images of you
along my busy street of moods
leave me a maker-image too,
but in life's dancing attitudes.

RUE SOLIMAN PASHA, CAIRO.

XVI

ELEGY II

Shop Window

In the confused magnificence of love
is no community, but unsharing crowds
of shuttered faces where no secrets move;
but a perpetual early-closing day.
The tender lust that sanctifies our bloods,
that flowered by companionship, the way
of the moth's mind, they neither feel nor speak,
haunted with flames: our world's a spirit-walk.

Behind the dreaming shutters of our faces
the spider fingers thoughts, and we dissect
with sharp artistic hands our gains and losses;
build the mosaic of a filtered world.
We hang a blinding arras upon the fact,
for wild wild unpardonably wild
the roaring of the outer enmity.
Yet we, being islanded, will draw down that sea.

Never believe us; poets tell you lies:
the burglar breaks the window, and the door
blows inwards, and the pictures tatter loose.
The snarler with hooked fingers, or the man
with nooses, throw a shadow on the floor.
Sooner or later we shall weep again.
There is no refuge from the teeming road
and the four walkers waiting to be God.

World was not built for dreams, my dear; the dreamer
cores his unsympathy to a navel of gold;
rides home at evening swathed about with clamour,
he in his inward starlight never seeing

commercial colours, or the nervous mould
that hangs their lightning round him. And so being
rapt from humanity, wake not till their feet
press down his bones to raise up Regent Street.

So our delight will never be alone,
or straight and safe as the lark's tower of air;
familiar things will break it, strange look on
with the fierce laugh of lynchers; and the sea
speak our end in mountains to the shore.
Oh if that future tears us, it will be
but bridal violence. For he loves you still
who leans and weeps upon the window-sill.

CAIRO.

XVII

COPTIC CHURCH

How far beyond the homes of sense
rears up this primitive pretence
of a transcendent flesh (whose birth
was from the centric monolith).
We bow the lintel of our head
to written lintels of the dead,
pictorial inmates of a room
cut in the frozen curl of time:
respecting older than belief
our greater ignorance of life.
Nor any faith beyond the brain
is more than a dark love of man.

So built within this frame of Christ
are stones of a remoter past:
the blazoned myth of Horus lies
within these faded images
where glowed Mithraic pigment in
the Thracian monks' symbolic line;
the spirit of this place is all
the dust of worship in the wall,
the worship of ourselves in God,
the blood's dark instinct from the dead,
whose memory of magnificence
reared up this primitive pretence.

MUSTURRUD.

XVIII

EGYPTIAN DANCER

Slowly, with intention to tempt, she sidles out
(a smile and a shake of bells)
in silver, tight as a fish's, and a web
of thin-flame veils, and her brown buttery flesh
(but she is a mermaid with twelve metal tails)
glimpsed or guessed by seconds.

Slowly the insidious unison sucks her in,
and the rhythm of the drums,
the mournful feline quavering whose pulse
runs through her limbs; shivering like a bride
she lifts her arms into a lyre; there comes
a sense of nakedness

as the red gauze floats off; and of release.
          She is all silver-finned:
it hangs from wrist and ankle, she is silver-
feather-crowned, tight silver across the breasts;
skirt of bright strips; and where in the fat forced up
          her navel winks like a wound.

The dance begins: she ripples like a curtain;
          her arms are snakes
– she is all serpent, she coils on her own loins
and shakes the bells; her very breasts are alive
and writhing, and around the emphatic sex
          her thighs are gimlets of oil.

All the half-naked body, as if tortured
          or loving with a ghost,
labours; the arms are lifted to set free
atrocious lust or anguish, and the worms
that are fingers crack as croupe or bust
          or belly rolls to the drums.

Wilder: the drift of the sand-spout the wavering
          curve of the legs grow a blaze
and a storm while the obsession of music hammers and wails
to her dim eyes to her shrieking desire of the flesh
that is dumb with an ecstasy of movement and plays
          fiercely the squirming act

and sweat breaks out she is bright as metal while the skirt
          spins like a flower at her hips
into the last unbearable glorious agony
between the lips and suddenly, it is over:
a last groan of the drum, panting she drops
          into the darkness of past love.

XIX

ELEGY III

The Convalescent-Party

A rakish summer with cocked leaf and flower
winks at the coloured walkers; the river
lolls, a witch's tongue, between the islands
and the swaggering shores.

Holiday: and the crows like old umbrellas
peck with a more Etruscan joy; the shadows
are poor relations on the lawn; light is
a dancing fearful thing.

The woman with the violet breasts, the child
in tartan, chair and flower-bed and building,
stand in a ring and leap like fire beneath
book-binders' heavens.

Tap-dance of tennis-balls; the smell of water;
the grumble of sad years in carnival:
and I stare through the party with a face
as hard as a head wind.

Sick sister, brother with the worm at heart,
you becoming enemy, or nothing,
oh all you fading people, with bodies
wrenched on the common ropes,

we with each other's envy like a mask
invent, remember, dramatize, to join
our sinister entertainment with ourselves,
plush lovers and wax laughers:

all you fading people, do you not feel
the flick of eyes, and the heart turning over,
the weather and the weather-makers in
your desperate countryside?

What are we doing with our garden, watching
the blown hair of the grass, and our false bodies
acting here together like hands pressed
upon a smiling mouth?

What are we doing with desire and hate,
unreal time and place, bad brilliance
reeling from light; the colour and the talk
that giggles and says nothing?

You, sitting in the blue ring of the sick,
blonde girl revoking on the ace of spades,
round you the folded wind presents ambition
and our dull grasp of sex:

though you become our symbol, and a future
with female days, the lace of dalliance,
sharp hands towards you, and a glassy clearness,
hold out this horror of

ragged bright-weather behaviour, season of
sun-trees; beaten heart of the pathetic
fallacy of mankind – who are the shadows
and the celebrations.

Vast in this poisoned gaiety impends
the writhe and shiver of love, and the shy bed
of new communion; darkened things that bite
like legendary birds;

the failure and the lack, the grin cut
on a face that will not own itself; the tiny
clapper at the core of our polite
soft fruit of sound and fury.

Oh for ourselves and you, this prancing day,
as hard as a head wind I set my face
against the power of something small within us
weeping and weeping.

ZAMALEK.

XX

SPHINX

He sends no voice, no secret, having none:
the face is mindless and unpardoning,
          we cannot gaze him down:
will not forgive that old high insolent stare,
the pointless aristocracy of enormous time
          withered in stone.

That he forgets; has let slip everything
but the hard spine, bred reflex of conceit;
          venereal turkey-tongue
of clamouring demotic emptiness
paints him as it is, in this fruity foreign south's
          beast-headed throng,

dead image of its degradation, mate
of ambiguous wicked caricature
          – deceit and self-deceit
of the mud-bubble: making and becoming

the beggar with the carved blank eyes, the withering
        fellaha with her pot.

There was a soul, and the smile curtained power:
the generations of the sand blew in,
        a horse's-tail of sour
sweat-knowing men, and wore the meaning out;
quenched, broke up like flies in a room, his pyramids'
        crowns of memorial fire.

On the hotel veranda for the moon,
past moving dimness elusive as a scent,
        the eye on their rough skin
sees them, and him beyond, through the wrong end
of the race: one hears, in the smack of hands on a stone flank,
        no secret, having none.

MENA.

XXI

CIVILIANS

For those who die in blood bruise and amazement,
all pity fails – the anger, the distress,
calmed or distorted, a dead face; appeasement.
Remote in the elaborate cage of chess,
a pencilling on maps, they cross no path;
honour but find no anguish in that peace:
honour the failing majesty of death.

For those who live in their anonymous power,
battering the darkness in the drunken streets
– the animal wild exhalation of war,

blind struggle of the soul in horrible nets
– what rage, who are the sparks of old men's wrath?
The proud violence and danger of their nights
honour the failing majesty of death.

As Arden's blood burnt on the rushy stone,
tongues are stained into us; you may know the knife
by which our dancing March has been struck down;
how jealously we died of our own grief,
pursuing easy bitterness with no faith!
But bled in epitaphs, memory, life,
honour; the failing majesty of death.

Not the imperial event, sky-chasm,
the open fury only windows feel:
we break the light within us, lens and prism,
cold brightness of an infinite withdrawal:
honour us also: you are grown our truth
who would be vision, would be light, and fail.
Honour the failing, majesty of death.

XXII

They know the lion's power,
being now indifferent,
whose eager limbs have learnt
to suffer without fear
or consoling love
the bridal and the bed
of the unearthly dead.

They lie in beds of love
with worn and vivid face,
where fall in one embrace

the dead by the alive
the carnal by the just,
being now indifferent
to lust or monument.

They have all grown just,
as mindless change or growth
– animal life and death,
blind blood of trees, thrust
of the innocent spray
and the pitiless flower:
they know the lion's power.

XXIII

ELEGY IV

"...on one side lay the ocean..."

Standing between the city and imagination
I hear the gravel of hurt faces whisper:
"We are the huge electrons of your passion:
  oh leave the mad canaries and the lilywhite boys
  for into the current there has crept disease;
  we are of radium, we are decaying stuff,
  thought as bent as a brook will sharpen angles:
  the little mole is dying of diseased love.

" See how the swarming harridan ferments in marshes
  of soft thighs, and the insistent sewer unfolds
  an aphrodisiac spindle; how the blushes
  of newborn lust anger the impending limb.
  There is no line or diver in the stream
  whose wild dolphins will not pause to save
  the gentle bridegroom cowering from the indignity,
  and the brutality, of achieved love.

" The unachieved is harder, though; when each confesses
into a darkness, into a serpent air.
Society is all its lonelinesses;
but you, or we, are haunted by the curing flesh
the poison body a despairing wish
for the broad arrow of kisses, for the knife
and prison of sexed hands. Have we an hour
not crying for the fullness of this confident love?

" Thunder's upon the wasteful brotherhood of men,
clouding your darling photographs, your creased
unhappy letters. If you turn again
towards your entowered happiness, the comfort of
dreams that for yesterday and unresolved love
work in the symbols of the mask and scorpion
– thunder's upon the beauty and the pleasure of that slim
nostalgic watcher among Englishmen.

" The little mole is dying. For the maniac song
curls in these gutters like a guilty blood;
and all the streets you answer and their echoes ring
with crooked nickel bells, a creeping wilderness
of commerce and of crushed unmeaning faces.
And the worse desolation of ourselves, our lives
between two substances: bringing you need
for the long chords of your concurrent loves.

" Tomorrows are all earth; but yesterdays return
unchanging now the bitten earthworm or
the creature with hurt hands: something is born
and everlasting in your lover's-transience."

Be still: I know the sweetness and violence,
the bitterness and splendour of your twisted motion;
I hear the patient gravel of a twofold love
between the city and imagination.

ALEXANDRIA.

XXIV

THE INCUBUS

The sea is beating on the stairs;
the room is wise with limbs; hers
clutch me with hands of candle-light.
And the webbed eyes of love are sweet;
and the soft lath of woman bears
a heaven's agonising weight.

The mole is trembling on the mound;
my nerveless arm is bled and bound,
weak apprehender, angry with
the fear of my unmaking death.
Still to my lips, my traitor mind,
aspires the patience of her breath.

Sad miracle of mind, that so
can break the serpent's wing, now
in the pale courts of her to be
distracted from her proper joy;
and love be powerless, although
upon the stairway beats the sea.

XXV

ELEGY V

A Descent into Egypt

My flesh is naked under the smooth green sheet
for my, and for the season's heat;
but there is no-one lying beside me. So I stare
along the suddenly unfamiliar

landscape of my body – little shire
that's miles away, and everywhere, and me
– till I dissolve into horizons, happy
    as wall, air, or tree.

The window is my uninhabited mile,
where sunning fears and pities coil
like adders, and the flies that stick and fizzle are
another love locked with another fear.
But I am not all glass, all rick and heather:
somewhere upon me, once found, Egypt is
textile of cities and navel-oases
    that sprout as milestones rise.

Here at least grows so familiar that
all individual strangeness leaps out
like a mistake in syntax: shapes and colours wrong;
clothes; and the public depositing of dung;
infants clad only in disease; beggars that cling
(balance and wag their one-and-a-half limbs)
to bars and ridges upon moving trams,
    and stink at us for alms.

Architecture: Moslem and mud and brick,
concrete flats, tripper's-resort eclectic
twelve pension-office-brothel stories high,
rubbing shoulders as the *dame soignée*
does with the sergeant's wife; the Old School Tie
with robe and ruby Fez-cap, and the troops
with khaki children queerly blowing bagpipes
    that cry like babies.

A camel in a bath; a walking man
masked in a lavatory-pan;
trees like a bunch of parrots, mandrakes, golliwogs;
starfish on trees – poinsettias; vermin, hatred of dogs:

the inconsequence of bargain catalogues,
all superficial images – none that lingers
growing – shallow on palms and swift through fingers,
    and sterile as closed cars.

All superficial images: the crescent-flags,
or women's quickly too-crossed legs,
ivy of sunlight breaking river and reflections:
slouching masts; the husky mewing tones
of the cane oboes; the bright-skinned balloons;
and always the thick smell and feel of dust
– cotton-dust money-dust sex-dust brain-dust; and worst,
    the very dust of dust:

which moiling and yelling pours even into the gardens:
the donkeys' terrible ant-like burdens
are vomited in squatting circles, dance with phallic poles
around the claps, the chanting. The dust trembles
under their sexy wriggles and capriols,
into the beams and eddies I see flit
as over lawns shifting and smooth with heat,
    on my green coverlet.

For sooner or later we must all become
our even temporary home,
as my body is stretched out into a countryside
and the home is Me. For too soon ended
is the colony of self: Egypt is pane and bed
on which – beyond which – you and I can dare,
careless of pity, careless of circling fear,
    to love each other.

ORMAN.

XXVI

Since I have written strange and arrogant words
in a warped age, leaning my head aslant
the clack and rustle of enormous birds,
the dry articulations of the ant,
to my and to my mistress' thoughts; but known,
and from within me known, the resonant
intensity of war that shouts them down;
and have been lover, malcontent, and clown:
the little feathers that eat anger grow
upon my hands and flutter at my lips.
The faces of the dead cried like a bell,
but in your stillness heaven shall turn homeward now,
beating the reeds with little water-drops;
and the taut spire be troubled in the well.

XXVII

FOUR LOVE SONGS

I. Dido
The sea forgets her masters: the seaman
turns from her flashing hair, her green eyes,
strips to the muscle for a harbour leman;
and smiles when he dies.

The land forgets the reaper: his sickle
burrows in strange corn, his tavern tale
is lewd with names of women who were fickle;
he laughs, he drinks his ale.

The air forgets her lightning: the thunder
dies in remoter valleys; the great spout
of spangling water, corn and sea pull under;
she burns, and there is drought.

II. Europa
Fierce from the stoking lech of spring,
dark bulls charge bellowing
their criss-cross night of owls and ghosts;
trains; or like planets curve and swing
with the sounds of stormy coasts.
Lackaday, lully lullay
A dragon hath borne my make away.

Sweet her body and most warm,
her scent of rose-geranium;
bitter the blue-lit shed, the smells
of cinder and of ghostly steam;
the empty ladder of the rails.
Lackaday, lully lullay
A dragon hath borne my make away.

His burly humming wheels are hands,
tell in the arches of their winds
a dim rosary of towns;
the symbol of their urgent wands
an iron mockery of man's.
Lackaday, lully lullay
A dragon hath borne my make away.

Little wonder if he could
but pause to snatch her maidenhood:
they found another continent.
Zeus himself and hardly stood
against so nice a form and quaint.
Lackaday, lully lullay
My make doth bear the bull away.

III. Poppy and Mandragora
There's hopeless traffic wailing as the roads run by,
and indigo is chilling all the uncompanioned sky;
the sad lamps lighting up till thirty-nine o'clock;
the blank walls waiting for the crowing of the cock:
with a star inside me and a spirit like a flea,
I have your ghost within the hand of mandrake me.

The past pours nearer like a film-star's face;
tomorrow is a mirror of the locative case;
the wind walks sideways like a nightmare crab in black,
and the streets huddle inwards for a grab at my back:
but with now inside me and with feathers on my knee
I wear your ghost about the land of mandrake me.

The black dog drew me up, the black dog died;
I let the daylight grow me till I reached your side;
witch time is over us like wet red loam,
and every coiling shadow is a spike running home:
but every shuttered window is a sun behind a tree,
and the blood of you is warm within mandrake me.

The crowds have weird-lit features with white statues'-eyes,
lift the rolling tongues of creatures that are dust and lies;
tremble the lights at the laughing savage sudden cock;
the pendulum is icebergs and it's thirty-nine o'clock;
but time is growing in me as a deep green tree
that's you its birds and sun and grass and mandrake me.

IV. The End of the Story
Put out the candle, close the biting rose,
for cock and cony are asleep; the sheep
in her secretive hills, with fleece at peace,
now lies enfolded.

The hungry sceptre-kissing mouth, the moth
behind the fingers, no more eat the night;
the rooting worm has crawled away from play
in his wet burrows.

Now the extremest joys are dreams and toys;
it's darkness in a vast full-tide abed;
over abandoned bodies time shall climb
like the black spider.

Give memory all amazing hours, all showers
or sharply pouring seas between the knees;
slack as a rope, the flesh is dull, and full
of its perfection.

And all that lately flashed and leapt is gripped
into a knot of symbols; all's grown small,
quiet as curtains: brave be this your grave,
and fresh your garlands.

XXVIII

FOLK SONG

Zero, the chaos and the root
        (Sister, come out of the cold wind)
One the male branch that bears no fruit
        (Sister, the slim rain is falling)

Enharmony of two, the maid
Three the planting of the bed

Four is the everlasting love
But adultery dwells in five

Six is God and Satan; seven
are the stairs that go to heaven

Walk immortal among eight
    (Sister, come out of the cold wind)
We are nine and nine is night
    (Sister, the slim rain is falling).

XXIX

SUNBATHER

Her body moves to its design,
and the instinctive dreams begin,
the child of woollen toys and wax
discovering consciousness and sex,
desire of colours and of sweets
dazzled by new and drenching lights.
The childish laws, the remote world
still half a womb, are now concealed
under the woman's thickening mist
about her; willow-pattern past
out-painted by a You-and-Me
and the memory of a Tree.

Already there is motherhood
in the hips or bending head;
a writhing mistress in her thighs
plucks innocence from hands and eyes.
For a double flower has burst
from the blunt unmoving breast,
and mysteries begin to dwell
in the newly-murmuring shell.
While the strange locks and windows make

the world romantic for her sake,
unrealized by thought and limb
her power and her anguish come.

The crooked X by which we met
and are again made separate
– atrocious alexandrine years
– has plunged us too among the tears,
learning to howl within ourself
for love's hereditary wolf.
But we have pity left, perhaps,
for the child before she weeps:
our first adulthood was a thing
of hesitance from nursery-song
– her trembling poise, her growing-full
– an adolescent by a pool.

MA'ADI.

XXX

PISCINE

Water has so long drunk up reflections
it is dissolved in them, is painted sponges,
thief of itself and them; the limb that plunges
has been drunk by endless fluid actions.

Two mirrors, corridor of intersections,
toss images like balls to the world's end;
touching or breaking planes are closed, are bound
to single selves or to mosaic fractions.

Floating upon parrot-coloured water,
over the stained tiles, catlike I watch
the luscious diver sign her arabic letter
through air and pool; this is their meeting which
(the types restored, the locus tied) must scatter
the infinite imagined depth of each.

HELIOPOLIS.

XXXI

HOLIDAY

Now the garlanded earth clasps
the golden streamers of her pole;
the planets like a peal of bells
swing lofty for heart's holiday.
Now in tingling hours like wasps,
fierce as the tiger's flaming skin,
earth and her companions sway
naked Salome to the sun.

Oh but there's thunder in this light,
and all the after midnight when
beneath the groaning of the Wain
the cocks crow at the seventh flash
because the moon rises late.
Then fear leaves no dark thing undone
– horrors that strain the velvet leash
– nor any hound whistled in.

But holiday shall bring the Ram
into the Scorpion's house of life,
teach the bright-feathered sun to live

till the malevolence begins.
The world and we pour into flame
a flesh that mocks the running air,
a spirit that is bells and suns,
a day that rocks the dancing spire.

MATARIA.

XXXII

BATHERS

They flutter out of white, and run
through the electric wind to bathe,
giggling like rivers for the fun
of smacking mud in the toes, of lithe
and sliding bodies like their own
– sharp rushes, good to battle with.

The child knows all delight to be
naked and queer as his own name,
foreign as being loved; but he
feels as a kind of coming home
the flags that slap his plunging knee,
and the cold stocking of the stream.

Coiling in wombs of water, bent
backwards upon the sheets of air,
his wand of sexless body lent
to all that was or casts before,
he strips to either element
a fœtus or a ravisher.

So gladly virgin rivers rush
down to their amniotic seas,
children of cold and glittering flesh
that promise harvest as they pass
panics of tiny fertile fish
in the fast pale of boisterous thighs.

XXXIII

CHILDREN

Seed sitting in the womb of twilight, in the sad
air vibrant with needles of the fountain, fear
grown wind or trees – these as if unreal children, glad
and losing brightness, fruit the soil must bear
small as the ticking of a watch, as silence, move
in what unsure vast envelope of love!

They have been sent, gifts or faint pleading letters (though
to be unopened) into the cold unbiddable night
– the dangerous, the tired time, the dim world of the old:
surely the tree grows weary of its fruit,
the womb of being closed, the child of ripening:
surely the fountain overflows the spring!

MA'ADI

XXXIV

PATHETIC FALLACIES

There in the speaking garden, in the rich
assurance of a natural rhetoric,
we made our truth: or gallant on the beach
with infinite failure – rock that beckoned rock
– we knew the sea had promises to break
more often than its argument confessed.
Here the protecting fallacy was lost;
here naked man shrank before nature's look.

Lady, for all, all we observe in you
of seascape or of garden speech, leaves bare
the loneliness man is and locks him in:

for what is human nature is not there,
or is his own belief, forced to be true
as friend or understanding or as man.

MA'ADI.

XXXV

Fearing to write but writing, as I wrote
but always feared, of love excessively,
at last I know love is not you and I
– the individual anguish or delight
locked in, the prisoner's or the lover's night.
A little glass pins down the burning sky;
there is no apex to infinity:
we are the gathered power, the spiral's heart.

The star and the burnt insect under glass,
sharing the fact, must share the word of flame;
there is no point less infinite than space.

Sun and electron, circles are the same:
if you and love outstretch no universe,
what shall I apprehend without your name?

XXXVI

A CAROL IN TIME OF WAR

My cards upon the mantel-piece
are full of winter sentiment;
the English love of amnesties
covers iron blocks with paint
that I may now receive
greetings I don't believe.

A night of neighing bells brings home
to each his little orphan faith;
late as ever, loud with shame,
the altruistic trumpets breathe:
yearly the world expects
a saviour she rejects.

Who may, in pastoral hope of this,
forget the roaring of the gun?
– where in fields and factories
the exhausted flocks are strewn
whose Bethlehem of blood
bears neither star nor God.

I send the usual anodyne
that flatters and propitiates
– the charity of Auld Lang Syne,
tokens, tips, the glow that greets
out annual shuffling of
sixpennyworth of love;

but celebrate, though distant now,
the season that shall conquer it
with steady bond of pen and plough,
song and organ-throated pit:
I summon to the earth
our own undying birth.

XXXVII

THE BIRTH OF CHRIST

After that vast possession it was she
lay in the dark, the strangely quickened womb,
and yet was nothing, no person; God.
Then from without, touched her amazed flesh
with hands, trembling, full of love and pity;
was everywhere so foreign: but a virgin.
Where the great wings had beaten with no pain
and the light, the light, only a small cold pulse
opened and shut like an eye; and the smooth breasts
were not erect or struggling; nothing; she
was like a cool bed newly made. Beside her,
night after night, the old man lay and would not
sleep for wonder; would not touch, for doubt
and terror, the girl's body stolen from him
and from the world by those invisible walls.
Soon she desired him and that unknown act

of human passion; her dark was tears,
and craving of the parted mouth, sharp waves
in the arrayed flesh: but he lay more still,
more distant, than a shy boy. So at last
only the shame was left; to be rejected:
I to be temple of divine seed, I
an old man's irritable lust refuses,
I who am dry with lust? This also was
the Hebrew dream, and was not: how shall God
swim in my scorned flesh that no man desires?
Nothing. Only my silent bed. And ageing.

The second month was leaning against wind,
clutched from the sudden blow, reeling in
confused and battering fingers. She knew.
No way out: a wild road to walk lonely:
the burden, pain, all to be borne; and no
way out: the motherhood of God; God growing
in the dark salt inward blood; fed with her soul;
two natures clasped and struggling in her, self
and an appalling vastness, a new world,
to bear from shrinking and in dissolution:
she the weak virgin, the soft wand of pity.

And the great roaring terror folded her.

Thenceforward he slept from her: Joseph, half
in stabbing jealousy of doubt, who long
ago heard her denial, doubting; half
with God's hand in his fear: and spoke with hatred,
with reverence or love; but always little.
She, like a string drawn tight with terror, yet
was glad to be alone: his presence gripped
too hard on tender places where the mind
had not its armour. So avoiding speech,
seen but unreal and intangible

to all, she wore in silence, like perspective,
her dedication to the endless waiting.

And wondered serpent things, when things of man
turned from her like a glass: for no-one came;
for nothing came. Would not the calm angel
speak in the rainy curtains or the dove?
No message, no protection? But a pulse
stronger and stronger in her numbness. Now
she was a cup, only a cup, with God
as wine within her; growing wine. And time
crushed her with new fear: Can time hate, time hurt,
so? Oh shelter this enclosed vine, let it
flourish and be fruit. And all her future
hung to that sweetness like a swarm of grapes.

In those unreal acres of her days,
Herod and Egypt – flight and foreign speech,
all the pursuing cloud, desert and strangeness,
and her clear image in the holy well
– lay dimly, the unfinished balance: and
imagination blindly groping towards
that legendary pain of birth. She was
no longer woman, but a symbol. All
were symbols: Joseph; God; and one to be.
But she desired no meaning. She observed
curiously and with wondering – not to call
love or hope – human children; and they seemed
as far as birds or jewels or as visions
from her life and the life within her, that
she could not picture like them: not a child,
separate in the sun. He was an hour,
a custom and a future way. An organ.
And inwardly that crouching fishlike beast
ripened through history and became a god.

A stirring: and her head lifted in joy,
gazing into unearthly distance; at
a white moon growing heavy. Oh strange moon
of women, gradual and proud, needing
no darkness, and not dead. Strange pride of women,
the body leaning backwards like a shadow
from a filled lamp, yet bearer of the lamp.
And moving slowly like a sleep-walker,
she felt the alien life beating beneath
in its close cradle, its world-cradle: different
from her quickened heart; not terrible,
but trembling upon terror; a world waking.
And the world's weight was majesty, was a still
pride; a smile, delicate and unthinking
as water-light. A deepening content.

Only a restlessness, the coming of
the Bethlehem road and Sinai, and the green
thin line of Egypt: longings for men's faces
half-understood, but formless. Yearnings for
gold, and myrrh, and frankincense; and unknown
water. For a music never heard.
She gathered thorns. The cold abundant earth
flowered, with her longing, to an empty grave.
She knew the trouble of desire; its breaking;
aimless desire that steals and cannot build,
and has no power of will. She was loose flame.

And all the past, inaccessibly calling.

The Bethlehem road was real. Her heavy body
forced on the slow too-swift way between
successive darknesses. But she knew nothing.
Day was a dream of infinite toil: night *was*
– limbs loosed from outrage, the thick excitement
mounting in her for the imminent birth,

and the vague nightmare of the journey: all
faded into the insistent life
already more intense than hers. To nothing.
Sleep. And one night was Bethlehem: three lives
beating at closed gates: for the warning clenched
her body like a fist. Again. She must
not yield. Again. Till, without knowledge, she
lay down between the animals: and waited.

Till the god fought in her like anger, and
her body fought; till her soul withered, that
this agony was not the end: but how
long? There was no time. Like a dying house,
all that was she, shook down. The heavy breath,
moaning, the gradual mounting of the scream,
were not of woman but inhuman flesh
unendurably fighting a blind power:
Ah world of pain; how shall this tiny body
hold you, that roar like water through me? Over
me: real as iron, moving the flesh like wind,
tearing the flesh like storm: grinding the soul.
Oh you enormous wind against out small
and yellow lights: infinite darkness moving;
oh heaven-striding cold, the dancing-floor
of merciless vacancy: oh be my garments:
I am alone: vast world and little walls
are weight upon me: oh unhelpers, distant
and never clearer – shelter, break through to me.
Ah but the crying! Was it that I cried?
This is no longer I: I am the pain
folding this wrenched and weaving body of
an unknown woman, crying. Oh thick harsh
anguish of the cries! Now. Could I save her,
out of the beating space about us, watching,
enemy: rolling the atrocious quern
of her torn body, and her staring thought.
No longer I; I could not endure…

Then passive suffering without thought; the patience
of animals. Long inarticulate pain:
pain like a wheel; red armour of the last
explosive swallowings into birth. Then only
an emptiness – such fierce and long reality
over – a lightness; and no memory.
Smooth with accomplishment, inert, she lay
and was a cool bed newly made: for it
was she brought helpless to the foreign air,
wailing: she had been born. The child was she.
He had come through the portal she alone
bore, among mothers: the last pang of birth
her bridal stab – closing one circle in
one point. She dared not look to see what stain
or imperfection marred his body: God,
her God, her child a monster, horrible.
Only believed him God, and waited for him.

And over his thin cry, the noise of angels.

TERENCE TILLER

UNARM, EROS
(1947)

WITH THE GIFT OF THIS BOOK

To hurt and fear, to every love,
doors will shut or disappear:
I stand in patterns on the floor,
closed in the fuming light, and live
          to hurt and fear.

The poem kills its ancestor:
whatever calls the hand, or fills
the mouth with suns and waterfalls,
words are the closing of the door:
          the poem kills.

Lights will not burn in their own smoke:
I have seen the dead return;
and where those hollow fires have been,
where lips were motionless and spoke,
          lights will not burn.

Smoke will not lie upon its flame:
volcanic day, when earth and sky
strode from each other, God lay
coiled in creation round his name,
          smoke will not lie.

But fire and death are in its tongue,
coiling in truth, shape without breath.
The latch is of a dragon's tooth:
we have seen little, being young,
          but fire and death.

SUBSTITUTES

Squeezing the private sadness until words
pearl round it, and all images become
the private sadness and the life; and a name
blood. Or flowering like a bride towards
the object, amorous of image, a home:
giving oneself to symbols; feeding myths.

There is one house beyond opposing paths.
Pelican or vampire is the same.

Only by going in and not around;
pulsing with stone's cold veins; duck's world,
    rock's world;
sifting the air as trees; long as the wind;
sucking the earth as wheat; become a field.
No myth will ever come to any good:
but biting the wasp's gentle apple; being blood.

SPRING LETTER

The earth turns over, our side feels the cold…

Lovely, but here no part of me, the world
rolls under shadow like a woollen ball:
all terror's darkening magazine, the cold
indecency of outward violence, will
grown lecherous with death, all crouching might
of iron, being far, even seems beautiful.

The wind's cold surplice in the sky, I sit
here, in the washed and choirboy afternoon;
and the grass claps its coloured fingers at
the clarity of water; and the sun
is in my hair like a chrysanthemum.
For here the will of quietness is done.

No, not of war: the dragon and the drum
that pulse his blood about the world are here
a breast beneath my hand, and out of time.
This tall season is my chanteclere
from night in mirrors, cannon flowering
like falling trees; all ceremony of war.

Calm acres and Mozartean air, spring
with its cold confetti in the boughs,
are not the world but a more inward thing:
as a wet garment on the body shows
the curl of limb and muscle, this day
droops in the shape of secret images.

Love, and the lovely clothing of its play,
its thinking film upon the flesh; the stride
and ache of afterthought to our long woe
our tenderness, the hangman of the blood:
here in your flowered scarf of Egypt, deep

as seasons under water, blooms our good.
A silkwhite skein of egrets that sew-up
the ploughman's gashes on a field: our words
have glittered so across a wounded hope
and been a splendid prophecy of birds;
and the wet crops that flourish towards sand
in growing wildfire, the childbed of seeds,

are in the planets' march to us, our end.
Oh infinite progression from our close-
cupped origin, acorn of stellar wind!
Here in the olive-shadows of our peace
is movement too intense for motion, heart
of a great tigerish whirlwind over us.

More terrible than fear, that bestial heat
rages beyond our vision and is safe:
iron insects with locked horns, the beat
of heavy air, horrible cells of life
that is not man but built of him; the smash
of wings and bodies; anger, dismay, grief:

all pain that makes a bugle of the flesh
turns here to awful beauty, beautiful
because our lives are under it. This hush
we know our love by, and our secret will,
is the exceeding clamour of the bat.
Then here I see our union grow full,

the wind's old scars and wounds cut into it,
a strip of hazel-shining foil, the river.
Fast in the river's darkening mind, I sit
and reach towards Europe, pitiful as a lover,
through this enormous shadow of the world,
while beautiful and remote, the world turns over.

Near Maadi, 1942

PERFUMES

Not every ghost has died before it haunts:
perfumes it seems have shadows, and will throw
days before them those thin beckoning scents:
unnamed, as the first sounds of poems grow
– formless and soft, like far-off instruments.

Mistily three days round me, blind men's trees,
changing as eyes, bodiless odours have lain:
the lemon-garden or the heat of bees;
November beaches' salt and iodine;
plushy church-air; lips' faint fragrances.

Now as the poem read, creating more
than word or reader were, grows firm and thrills
like a cello between thighs, the form is here:
your perfume round me like the death of bells,
and you moving the sweetness of the air.

Because our hands trail in each other as though
a child's through water, and refuse goodnight,
I carry perfume back with me, and you,
your body the bell's singing heart: the sweet
perpetual ghost again; but this time true.

HANDS

Eyes are the spoken word, but dark
will make them silent, where
the lovely shapes of rhetoric
have no-one left to hear.

A body built into an arm,
and the blood shouting, still
though passionate as heat, is dumb
like a kind animal.

Of seven kisses that have speech
in characters or times,
none is a messenger of much:
they only tell their names.

Hands are like letters to be read
in braille or fire; they light
the body that becomes their road,
the mind they re-create.

Subtle in mood or motion, they
are thoughts of silent men;
and able messengers, to be
not-thoughtless for their own.

They that carry everything,
learning and thinking, look
past one another to the tongue
within, that will not speak.

The body in its amorous belt,
or eyes and lips that meet,
know nothing that they have not felt,
say nothing they forget.

And darkness the girl-eater has
no power upon them: give
to lust the subtlest of his ways
– only the hands can love.

FACE

Her soft lines over subtleties of bone
read like a script meaning itself alone;
we can add nothing but our own unrest.
          Perfection is at last
the death-mask of refusal to be more:
humanity as animal or flower,
   a face that cannot be undressed.

There is no more to say of it than "beauty",
than the dumb word. Creation, journey, pity,
the powers behind speaking loveliness,
          starve on its shallow glass
– the shell that mirrors what it cannot hold.
There is nothing here that has been old;
   and we say "beauty" meaning "loss".

ROMAN PORTRAITS

There has never been a naked face;
perhaps ghosts or angels have it, or the dead
whose images outlast them: but bare-eyed,
the mouth only a mouth, the lines untied,
is not a living face: faces wear moods for dress.

The mask, its artifice of power or grace,
thought led by the masker across wood,
metal or paper, is the shell of a mood
stripped off and living: the mask does not hide,
but chooses limits, being chosen to express.

I have seen the lineaments of a place
unmask suddenly as a rising bird;
a torn-out page: so human faces could
lose their bright meaning plaster, and have died
into an echo's firm impersonal absences.

These masks and statues of an ancient race,
expressive bandages for limb and head,
living on history, like a fallen god,
were greater than the hollowness they hid.
What is it now speaks through their mouths, looks through their eyes?

FEAR

Now it is time for building houses: when
the beast shall speak to his landscape and be beckoned,
and all trees shout and leap at us, and men
be towers running: night around us reckoned
by belting winds, faces and bodies breaking
dangerous ways into each other: fear
in the streaming field, rage in the air,
and the anger of the wicked bell awaking.

Time to use doors: when trusted objects crouch
always behind us; horror in the bed,
or smiling at windows; eyes as deft as fencers.

Time to tie cities down and trap the watch.
For now that evil rides upon his blood
the beast speaks, and the alien landscape answers.

HOSPITAL

The heavy mask of heat was lifted; here
the cold stone smelt of colleges, and all
moved quietly and strangely as a star:
silence one broke, daring to be or feel.
    And then the flowering of your room, as if
    out of a dream, or from a future life;
and speech as hard as if at a farewell.

Selves were intruders behind time or glass:
no vision, yet a stranger, smiled at me;
and common things were like an alien Mass:
the ritual of talk, of cake, of tea,
    world's acts and images, were all pretence
    – living in history, and pathetic, since
unreal, like a wedding of the sea.

Oh strange and shuttered, being masked in being,
mask in mask; where, like strangers in a lift,
pity and love looked on, nor dared set blowing
the cold winds of emotion or of gift.
    Glass garden, and a sweetness not to break
    with nakedness of stripping earth from rock,
where past was violence, and future theft.

Pause at the door was knowing which was true:
summer was helpless as a foreign guest.
Here was assurance, your whole world and you
as warm as fruits: the white fig of a breast,
    your private family of dolls and roses,
    and the last image, breasts of grapes like bruises.

But parting was as if two portraits kissed.

Gezira

THE LAWN

Through the hive-quiet of the afternoon
and its unpausing sun, eyes full of the sun
upon deep hair coiled like a lamp to watch:
here each to each
held minutes out like hands
when even little things were friends.

Excellent union of content: the warm
and priestly air of winter moving calm
as friendship over us, and no cold breath
of corners; both
like garden things, brought near
by easy and unpassionate care.

And under images the words peeped out
of the mind like mice, undaring (showing-white
of pleasant shoulder from the sleeve stripped up;
intimate shape
of limb and body and stance;
paper and laughter, mood or sense):

out of our cage and weaving of small things,
our tree of talking – oh what other tongues
silently flashed like birds; what faster curve
of blood – to love
or fear – woke in me all
my strong unseasonable will!

Zamalek

BIG CITY

Crossing of strangers among lights
while cold and secret through the streets
we run on homeward wheels, and learn
a no-man's-land of flesh and bone.
Homeless the rolling blood that cries
of love and Love in hidden ways
where kisses like a bird fly back
and bring no bounty to their Ark,
since all about the city stands
night, like a monument for friends
whose lives in hills of darkness share
the serious motions of desire,
passion that estranges all
but the involuntary shell
and clings to nothing in the gulf
but the blind magnet of a self.
Our sense has only sense for light
and the flames are separate
while among them aimless words
have no home to move towards.
Once on a murmuring afternoon
speech was a dancer in the sun,
while cold as whips under the grass
the secret plants crawled up to us
who now are in their pulsing dark
while the dancer stamps us back
– a flower and a root that strives
towards it. And a god who grieves.

Cairo

BEGGAR

Old as a coat on a chair; and his crushed hand,
as inexpressive as a bird's face, held
out like an offering, symbol of the blind,
he gropes our noise for charity. You could build
his long-deserted face up out of sand,
          or bear his weakness as a child.

Shuffling the seconds of a drugged watch, he
attends no answer to his rote; for soul's
and body's terrible humility,
stripped year by year a little barer, wills
nothing: he claims no selfhood in his cry:
          his body is an age that feels.

As if a mask, a tattered blanket, should
live for a little before falling, when
the body leaves it: so briefly in his dead
feathers of rags, and rags of body, and in
his crumpled mind, the awful and afraid
          stirs and pretends to be a man.

Earth's degradation and the voice of earth;
colour of earth and clothed in it; his eyes
white pebbles blind with deserts; the long growth
of landscape in his body: as if these
or these dead acres horribly gave birth:
          here will fall from him like disguise.

Only a sad and humble motion keeps
the little space he is, himself: to row
his mindless caves with ritual hand and lips,
and wonder dimly at his guilt: with no
memory of it now: it was perhaps
          too fearful, or too long ago.

Giza

CAMELS

I see them swaying their strange heads like geese,
nineteen camels in a string like geese in flight;
as if approaching a problem, or in quest
but baffled a little, a little unsure of their right.

But I am glad their supercilious look
sees as I see the powdery town, the tall
activity of streets, the buttoned-up faces,
the cars like secret agents, the want of it all.

Gentle and sure as pianists' hands, their feet
deliberating on the stone press out
in rhythms that have nothing to do with us
the coins of their aloofness in scorn or doubt.

The motion of the blind or the very proud:
they could be blind; but where their masked eyes fall
they have the sailor's distant and innocent gaze
for where this ends, for the limit and want of it all.

Helwan

FLYING TO TRIPOLI

Pages of sand; the slow black tape of road;
hills with salt and wreckage in their laps;
the canvas Mediterranean a guide
to windy Tripoli and the listing ships.
It is a kind of death, this vanishing:
the country or the flier? Blue flight; then
after oblivious landmarks, fall with dipped wing
like angels and with power, among men.

Down by the harbour over drooping wires,
on amazed marble bathers in the bowl,
the gloating of the sun is drops or flowers:
the oleanders and the fountains fall.
And what is real enough to touch? – we who
have died so fast along the death and fire,
following where we cannot possibly go,
dazed by the violence of that mine of air?

Oh flowery white and military town,
gapped like a boxer's mouth and pink with trees;
twirled by the ugly finger of the gun,
a restless bowl: or with dogs' humble eyes
upon the quiet coarseness of a rein
strong enough to be gentle. Where the lulled
ships nestle deeper; masonry scuttles down
from gash or scaffold; houses have been killed.

Flags that shrug and huddle in the wind,
summer of war, colour of tree and sky,
break us your angry bread; and for this land
that swarms with supplication not to die
– hunger of withering spaces where the crops
are dragged like salvage sunwards; of men and hills
with death with salt with wreckage in their laps.
And for this town of hesitating walls,

the injury and shyness of a guilt;
four eyes askance, held steady like a house
by dug-out, buttress, rifle, barbed-wire-belt,
where all turns downward, sweet and ruinous:
beauty that paints and wavers; fall of men;
dropping of strangers from enormous heights;
soft imprisoned terror in the sun.
Death and living have torn down their gates.

And agony ended here: dream into dream
by water-clock and flower-clock; rest with
the grey quay curving like a lover's arm
and as unsure. Pattern of peace and wrath.
For the guns tell the time: the earth falls
roaring and flowering from us; we are huge:
the tiny quilt of camps and farms and hills;
the road of urgent news; the turning page.

1943

FLARE

Suddenly the flare dropped. The buxom hills
curved over backwards, fell open like a book,
swam up to meet it. The white roadside walls
sharp as a denture, bars and masses of black
behind the vast hard light, the vaster ring
of blindness, lay steely in the frightening
silence of a picture or a clock.

Clear as if airless, a moon-landscape; only
no saintly idiotic planet's face,
earthlight; but hot and horrible and lonely
that flower-sailing eye in menacing glass.
Beneath it, the earth stirring without lamps:
the awful breathing of a thousand camps;
the probing gun; animal watchfulness.

Death's haunted stables and the gunner's star:
oh Bethlehem again – *and what rough beast*
in a night wearing ceremonies of war
hid like a guilt? No singing on this coast;
no mercy in the impersonal honest sand
whose (the flare vanished) briefly open hand
shut suddenly to darkness like a fist.

Homs - Tripoli Road

LECTURING TO TROOPS

They sit like shrubs among the cans and desert thistles
in the tree's broken shade and the sea-glare:
strange violent men, with dirty unfamiliar muscles,
sweating down the brown breast, wanting girls and beer.
The branches shake down sand along a crawling air,
and drinks are miles towards the sun
and Molly and Polly and Pam are gone.

Waiting for my announcement, I feel neat and shy,
foreign before their curious helplessness,
innocence bought by action, like the sea's amnesty:
all my clean cleverness is tiny, is a loss;
and it is useless to be friendly and precise
– thin as a hornet in a dome
against the cries of death and home.

How can they be so tolerant – they who have lost
the kiss of tolerance – and patient to endure
calm unnecessity? They have walked horror's coast,
loosened the flesh in flame, slept with naked war:
while I come taut and scatheless with a virgin air,
diffident as a looking-glass,
with the fat lexicon of peace.

The strangeness holds them: a new planet's uniform,
grasped like the frilly pin-ups in their tent
– something without the urgency of hate and harm,
something forgotten.
But that is not what I meant:
I should have been the miles that made them innocent,
and something natural as the sun
from the beginning to everyone
though Harry and Larry and Len are gone.

Coastal Battery, Tripolitania

ARMISTICE

In from the chintzy garden and the glare
he finds her in the cool cave of the room
straightening vases by the coloured hair,
patting the poll of a chrysanthemum
whose sentimental face nods back to her.

Collected. But the great gong of the heat
to which wild-rooted people blaze like a curtain
is passion of liberty in male sun and root.
He nestles in the vase, and has forgotten
all but her firm caressing of his heart.

Unarm, Eros: fighting love is over,
in from the battle, drinking through a stem
female charity for a flower or lover.
No more struggle, as hands or scissors come,
against possession or the power of the giver.

Abandoned now to love, but no more summers
– enslaved for all the rest – we turn to look
at those who fought in love with hate like swimmers
in lava towards love to a white rock:
to Hero's vase.

Peace to the tents and rumours,
peace to the amorous air on sea and farm,
and lovers grown each other's superstition,
and all poor earth above the joy of the worm.
Only immortal longings are compassion:
a woman and a flower: Eros, unarm.

THE VASE

Slowly the roses bleed into the water
a wound, a garlanded mouth, in every stem;
a languid sweetness turning rich and bitter
– the last of Rome.

Fragile and wistful as the weather, caught
naked and cold in flowers, with the grace
of virgin dancers, is the apricot
in our blue glass.

Barbarian slaves: the grounds where roses grow
are wild and thorny in their flaunting weeds;
where, stripped for wind, the flowering trees bow to
their green brides.

Oh trees in your arms lulling the wind;
roses written by the sun, your open lips:
to what imperial splendour are you bound,
and by what hopes?

Crushed in the beauty and the liquid noose,
you dance the apricot, draw the slow breath
of roses dying like Petronius
a seemly death.

DOUBLE WEATHER

Stiff mask of gold, the firelight pressed
like fever on my face: I lay
watching the weather be undressed,
the stormy bridal of the day.

But clouds that streamed with riches were
rocked in the wind's enormous wash:
their only touch was troubled air
– a distant voice, a lightning flash.

The river and the restless tree
lay in each other's eyes, and shone:
the diving bough untakeably
the wave too far to lean upon.

Passionate on bloodless glass
image and view came fingering
the mirror neither side could pass.
But in the weather's writhe and sting,

bare as the glitter of the pane,
a world of dubious light looked through
the pale surrender of the rain
and the embrace of striding blue.

I wore the heat like armour; she
like the wind's enfolding weight
and let a stream of hair fall free
towards the whispering of its light.

IMAGE IN A CEDAR TREE

Birds in the cedar, fluttering without a song:
early-lilting love and its philosophy
silently trail delicate aged wings among
the green December chapels of their cedar-tree.

The minaret, many-laced-and-leafed, the painted age,
is not more whole and wasted more contained a thing:
not here, not still, among the stone and the foliage,
is there a structure to shed leaves, be shared, or sing.

What should the cedar sing? Oh dumb brown throats,
oh airless wings, what ecstasy works unheard
now nothing is left wiser than the power of thoughts,
nor love beyond the singing of a bird?

BALCONY

Here in city shadows, under the bells,
here between chimes and the strong hammering street
clinging, like swallows upon smithy walls,
ten feet of tiling and an acre of night
our own, we cannot feel how incomplete
how overhung how loose love is. A wing,
a brassière of tiled steel, holds our wall tight
– balcony, balcony, bearing the world's wrong.

Behind us, and in all these thousand cells
(dark houses blazing to a field of wheat)
food, colour, character (and on them falls
the same embracing lonely orange light)
– the day's intentions and its fragments meet:
and life becomes a centred intimate thing.
How can you prove them pitiful but right,
balcony, balcony, barring the world's wrong?

Enemy water out of strangers' wells
floods to the heart on tiny dagger feet:
a thousand pointless hearts: grief in the halls
where sad tomorrows build their stalagmite.
Around them image and emotion beat,
and the rock winces from the swell and sting:
is the flood safe, or only out of sight,
balcony, balcony, bridging the world's wrong?

For love is not what the dark chime foretells;
and there is no assurance in our sweet
self-behind-armour, as of animals;
no festival in all this flowering height.
Lift up your barrier, let us sit and eat;
(*Love bade me welcome…*) give us grace to sing:
balcony, balcony, bearing the world's wrong,
the city bears no music. But it might.

Cairo

AUTUMN LETTER

Panting and flaring in the sun and wind,
immense and vastly purple is the bush we sit behind;
with a Dutch doll's-house pattern, pool and bed,
before us, orderly in green and gold and red;
and lesser bushes handing like windy wigs.
A child incessantly crawls and chuffles between my legs,
playing trains, and talking of tunnels with a gusty tongue,
and knows that purple is royal: I am king,
and our fierce-flowering shelter a palace, to which he crawls
– driving his little engine through the palace walls.

In his flexible ungoverned world, there is
no image for the convent of our hierarchies,
or switches between so and not: the politics
and springs and symbols of his playing – labour and sex
– are shadows for us in a caste of action:
this battling garden is not war and resurrection
until we lie. For him, the multiple
can be at once, and one, not known, and real:
his blond slender play-voice foretells and belongs
to a lover's agony and the ruin of kings.

And we are friends if now I do not save
a part of me that plays, if now I also live
created fact; commanding all that bows and blooms
to candelabra-courtiers in a thousand rooms;
living my knowledge that not a king but has found his way
troubled by a mislaid woman or a boy,
or overbearing labour – some love or weariness.
Or I must burn my signals in the trees,
and on my walls, and where tables and bushes kneel,
to an extraordinary chamberlain of steel.

For his strange doubt of selfhood is a sign:
all his unconscious symbols are awake, and mine:
obsession with bed or birth, with love or fear,
double pretence, and this bright breathless garden, are
ourselves, are you and I.
                    Struggling and creeping North,
now I can name you Love from a child's mouth,
and Here, and all our wistful years: a woman and
her poet, dancing and flowering in the wind,
who like a beggar must stand here and sing
for a child's affection, and hours gone too long.

Maadi

THE PHOENIX HOUR

Do not expect again a phoenix hour…

Grasp without hands, tell without lips, possess
utterly, without ceremonies of sex:
wedded like rays beneath a burning-glass,
clever and bodiless.

But love be many in surfeitings and lacks,
the brittle fury of the act, and in
all flowerings of your wild swans' marvellous necks:
until the heart learns locks.

Not love be amnesty (Love be alone
in Thebaid hours) nor man's magnificence:
oh inaccessible bird whistling to stone
death to this dirty town.

For love and Love are not alike in tense.
Twinning of blood by certainty is true.
Society is disobedience,
present but nowhere hence.

I have made this in charity for two
– hysterica caritas mounting towards the voice
– seeing the lonelier way out for you,
but nothing else to do.

EPITHALAMION

How far returning, that all strangeness seems
near and familiar as a mother; this creation,
perfecting woman, like the child's warm stillness;
a memory of confidence. Our loves are wombs.
Not the strange touch and unknown arcs of passion,
lighting and yielding of the body, break this fulness.

And not the wide anxiety, nor pain
suddenly shouting like a joy, and being joy:
it is the body that forgets the body
– tenderness somewhere in the dark and love like rain:
oh earth glad earth beneath him, agony
of being happiness, and other, and held steady.

New and impossible again; as if
a boy's thought lived, discovery again, and wonder:
terror of power forgiven, and room for pity,
love being harbour, being cloak or hand or knife.
Oh carrying of comfort, hurt of this tender
moulding of One to Other, violence of beauty.

All the flesh crying crying heart transfigured
now, like the splendid bitter lion of the sea:
the power that loses us: we are its breathing,
homeless and kindless as the wind, and blood-beleaguered.
She in the fierce *away* I have made be,
myself, her huge intensity of one and nothing.

World like a mist a ghost returning, room
slowly about us rising through our webs of night,
burden again of knowing, give us peace.
Each now for ever is the other's coming-home,
a shining archway quivering to that
infinity which swept us with its terrible eyes.

IMAGE IN A LILAC TREE

Tireless budding and flowering of women
to a child and a child; the closed evening-care
of motherhood: from what slim boughs the lilac
swells into lavender torches, the flesh
          blooms through its leaves!

Or now the heart is heavy and sweet with words,
and a great wind sways the tongue: oh eloquence
of gardens bursting through the narrow pen
into five senses, that clutch beauty as
          a child the breast!

The lilac's evening-coloured breasts of smoke,
bare like a Cretan lady's to the firm
poetic moonlight: love, conception, birth,
where the five tongues of living drink, and are
          poem and image.

BEFORE CHILDBIRTH

Miles without refuge for us, the night full
of strangers and remembering ways. The rain,
that makes all intimate, softly lets down
her glassy hair, and is a bride of steel.
Now this waste of city and our chance,
the golden-dappled sleeping animal,
blunts the wet wind and is innocence;
turns into love, for dark is its defence
and, in its breath, our sore defences fail.

We cannot count the dangers of tonight:
those dragon-haunted fields between us, where
iron rages against rain and air
and even our love, being naked, blows about;
treason of body, or of child; or luck
a frantic lion echoing in the street:
we give, tonight, what cannot be caught back
– the sadness and the trust, ourselves who look
past hopeless acres for each other's light.

Oh dark defend you, whom I love, and fill
with shining symbols the bed's dangerous lap,
and have begotten you on your sleep
quiet as a little home, a bell
though resting that calls distances together.
We open arms into the death of will:
soundless within, shadows and echoes gather
out of the poem, out of the pain, out of the weather,
the living refuge for us, the night full.

THE CHILD

All night they have been wounded on each other,
the waves that fall like armour from their poise
of leopard or of slingsman, and the trees
alive with arrogance and rage of weather.
We listen: not to ask what anguish drives
the wind through monstrous dark, what marriage brings
tumult and labour and the war of things:
these were the place and symbol of our loves.

There is no loneliness like birth: perhaps,
being aloof in pain, tonight is birth.
But not for you, whose world is kind, and sleeps.

When you have heard the meaning of the wind,
what will the symbol or the place be worth?
The world in which we made you is not kind.

THE UNBORN DAUGHTER

The suns return and fall, the seasons rhyme.
She holds the mastery of a lunar beat.
To her the gift of loving is in time.

Blood is the map and will be paradigm;
arterial red the rope upon her feet,
the sun's return and fall, the seasons' rhyme.

No cannon or no bell may call to prime,
no tower's march upon the pool be sweet,
to her; the gift of loving is in time.

Star in the blood that rings her only chime,
keep in the amorous air, and let your heat,
the sun's, return and fall, the seasons rhyme.

All that is now ambivalence or mime
will stay the last necessity to cheat:
to her the gift of loving is, in time.

Still coral, tiger, and about to climb,
she is born by the slow agony of wheat:
the suns return and fall, the seasons rhyme:
to her the gift of loving is in time.

SONG

A poem for a minute
for the embracing smiling
light upon a planet
sown flower swelling
where there is no time being
waiting or double seeing
is the budding of bells
in the happy pulse.

And silver-glass for bodies
in bodies soft embracing
for the flower the word is
the stream of mirrors kissing
there being no time being
waiting or double seeing
where the seconds curl
in garlands from their scroll.

Every word a mirror
a watershed shining
jewel and giver and wearer
the difference of joining
being made no time being
waiting or double seeing
carry the poise of pearls
or crystal-pulsing hills.

DETECTIVE STORY

I

My face was pale and dry and watermarked
as banknotes; my thin hands upon the tape
tore the hard mouths of companies; I cracked
the transatlantic cable like a whip;
a dozen Bourses trembled when I talked:
I did not want to die: I was twenty years old
with a house in Mayfair and a figure like a diving champion
and hair like Veronica Lake's but a deep shade of gold
and a clean fiancé with a moustache and a heart like a lion
and just about enough sense to come in out of the cold:
and really, my dear lady, if, when young
– as which of us was not? – you were... unwise,
perhaps, is kinder... some malicious tongue
might bring it to your husband's (ha! ha!) eyes:
he might, *you know, consider he'd been stung:*
but no desire of death: grey Gothic arches,
like learned eyebrows, were my natural home;
the book was ignorant as belief in witches;
primly above it in my celibate room,
I tortured it to death with needle-touches.

After the novelty of being dead
– the horror on the mat and in the well,
the lovely naked body on the bed
– after the shock, and slyly watching all
their mouths and gestures: then I knew it good:
a knowing corpse, with secrets; more than that,
the mockery; and more than that, the pride:
safe in the centre, the star-turn – and what
machinery at work because I died,
the burly fuss that follows death about!
So all my servile companies, the flash
of my enamel eyes, my proofs of sin,

my cold angelic learning, all my wish
for power and the reverent voice, seemed thin
beside the mastery of my helpless flesh,
its knowledge and its glory – but no trouble
ever again to take: even now
taunting the surgeon with my breasts, and able
to quell intruders with cathedral brow
or send a shudder down the toughest cable.

II

For it was you I killed: the weeping itch
of being nobody, ignored in love,
no latimer, a coward and not rich;
of knowing I was really good enough
though things went hot and silly at my touch.
You stole my lover: now you would know better.
My front-page hero (you're there now all right)
you laughed at me: I do my laughing later.
You kept me, like a dog: but I could bite.
You drank champagne: how is it under water?
For I was brave and clever, having found
nobody's knife and altered all the clocks;
shot you in darkness and was hard to find
– your body, cuckolded by stairs and locks,
left, like insulting excrement, behind.
Plans: the defiant presence, the sneering
alibi, or the motive in the false
moustache: all beautiful, a joy preparing,
proof against proof, infallible – or else
the final wonder of my disappearing.

And it was you I killed, who bred my germ
of being less: my lustful father, hated
in every herald bed-spring; the white worm
that coiled me to my mother; the excited

sneer of the schoolmaster who meant me harm
with an erotic birch. And it was I:
self-murder of self-loathing, the one act
I knew I could overbear and justify,
at worst escape, or drown, that I had lacked:
and when I killed you, both of us would die.

But, improvising fugues, and playing chess
blindfold on fifty boards, I felt my power
– the maze and blinding logic of the chase:
gambit enfolding gambit: subject, fear;
the inner voices answering, success.
And even trapped – one castle weak, one chord
left unresolved, the falling fabric certain
desired and known – I could be reassured:
last, sweetest wrong; but pride before the curtain,
having the right, the just and final, word.

III

Then, swift behind the stage, my third disguise:
hard-helmeted, and blind, and indolent,
learned on bells and the behaviour of grass,
the playboy with the famous instrument,
the spinster with an attic of old brass:
I entered from the other side. How soon
the hidden truth stood bare and burly, snarled
spider-web grew straight and lethal twine!
Praise Eton, Girton, praise the underworld,
Freud, logic, intuition: praise my brain.
I used the Encyclopaedia for my lens;
I twisted handcuffs from a village scandal;
found syllogisms in the rarer wines,
and saved the hero's life by liking Handel.

Frequent and baffling as a list of trains,
(facts in each other's arms, lies like equations)
ruins and ore of knowledge were my task.
I was the man who memorised the stations,
the girl with guineas as her lightest risk,
her honour pared like nails by Limehouse passions,

who thought with razors and was pure of course.
I was the poor policeman with the kicked
but highly Hendon intellectual arse,
never allowed impatience, never licked:
I was the dogged mystery in Morse.
I who was puzzled by my children's nature,
to whom my wife was Nabatean script
and every human word an overreacher
(and crime and commerce happened while I slept)
– was now the gently-smiling tolerant teacher
dandling the dirty world. This world was clear:
the echoes answered and the paths led home;
facts were a fit, like sexes; lies were
swathed and unwieldy as a hammered thumb;
and even failures were Neaera's hair.
Myself, because I needed to be God,
I killed and caught: the child's ambiguous life,
the penny spinning, dreams of being dead,
the worlds that intersect along the knife,
terrible and released.
All this I read.

READING A MEDAL, AND OTHER POEMS

(1957)

READING A MEDAL

who, minter of medallions,
casting or striking, caused me so
to speak with double voice in bronze,
I may not help and cannot know.
But I am Pallas, and I bear
the mask of war by wisdom; you
shall spin my olives to despair:
all my reverse will say is true.

(*Turn me, and read that other side;*
you must return: for, mask and coin,
I give no rest unless you ride
the felloe where my faces join.)

My face is Aphrodite's – she
that rules by myrtle and by dove;
I loose my zone to let you see
the end of reasoning by love.
Nothing my obverse tells is true:
turn till you read me as it was;
turn till you know me, and renew
my helpless paradox – because

FOR LOST LOVERS

Next unto this Planete of love
The brighte Sonne stant above...
(John Gower: *Confessio Amantis,* vii, 801 – 2)

The sun stands in the abyss of giving, and gives;
all in his corridor among the receding stars,
the vaporous yield of the field of wildfire, lives
by his yielding. The keen path of Mars,
Earth's powdered highway upon emptiness,
and Venus' glittering zone, hold from his deep
music of bounty, balance of duress
by which together being spun they sleep.

Standing where all is well, he draws to him
by gravity of love what else would lie
rolled in those flying caverns on whose rim
of segregation they both seek and fly
the ardour of possession – and yet swing
forever home; neither can reel nor break
their tense their singing distance; they must sing
to the racked windlass and the vibrant lake.

For every broken coupling lashes hard
even in breaking, the act, the memory
of its united strains: there is one chord
by which all planets and all stars are free
in consort who would die in unison.
Follow the paths of the receding stars:
even the centre of your light is one,
and may not turn aside to follow yours.

TROPICAL AQUARIUM

The twisted many ribbons, the absurd
flexes of small and coloured flesh, alive
but marginal in error; the web-stirred
weave of a tiny spectrum: though I gave
a home of delicate green hair, of wet
warm growing little forest, now upon
a choking emptiness they writhe and beat,
dying of air on the November stone.

Young and inordinate and gauche, an arm
brought diamonding down that measured thing:
they know dimensions now that are not warm,
those pained sick projectiles. In the wrong
cold and excess and lack, in the mad space,
they die of being taught – by accident
of being taught – whose logic of light grace
had been a closed unseason sunned through flint.

They will not be a poem now again:
the amnion is broken. Though a child
is building-up the common double pain,
it will not be those children (for the sealed
thought was not sterile) but a spawn of things
tided, with young legs, on a desperate rim.
Must I be glad, having seen them lose the wings
that swam with rainbows, rainbows floating: them?

THE BIRDS

When, drawn behind his lamplight and shut doors,
his windows dumb and his day carpeted,
the miser contemplation glowers within
his jealous web (and winding silence pores
on toys of Nothing in that golden shade),
or falls to mapping knowledge by the coin,
or counts himself in poems; when he stands
in his own image on the glass of prayer:
whatever asks a secrecy of hands,
or wedded patience of the tower of cards,
his wild familiars trouble; he will hear
the mouse-eyed amorous eavesdropping birds.

Oh birds whose homely wings flutter his pane,
cry back your brothers on the weather's wing
wrestling in red air, tassel-hovering, twined
in the blue patterns of the shoals of sun;
cry back the whistle of their flight, their song
in the torn evening trailing like threads of wind.
He knows their picaresque employment; he
has watched from the wife-lintel of his door
that eloquence of breath, and how the tree
streams bowing through its amethyst: but all
his care and cunning have been bound (no more
those echoing coloured miles) within the wall.

THE EPITAPH

'Where have you come from? What do you want with me?'
'I am the poem you have so often killed
with careless books, or booze, or accidie.
Be sure my ghost is with you: has it not filled
every blank end-of-chapter? waved and sighed
in every waiting silence – and been heard?
But this is all of me that has not died:
Oh my deliberate white bird'.

'What do the words mean? I must understand
or cannot write'. 'Have you forgotten? How
shall I recall the bone I died-from, and
the image of my birth, who am ghostly now?
Was it on black or green field? or flung high
into the dazzle of air? or snatched and slurred
by the grey and leap of wind on what lost sky,
oh my deliberate white bird?'

'I have no picture. Was it a bird at all,
or (not a dream, I think) some girl, desired
and –' 'Were they many, and so casual?
– to fade upon a ten-years-not-required
sweat-crumpled page torn out? Live only so:
Oh my deliberate (upon that word
the graining of an inky thumb) and no
more epitaph than a faint *white bird?*'

'Then you were dead even before I wrote:
lie still; I have destroyed your epitaph'.
'Now all of me, with clamorous feathered throat
and arrogant wing, or appleblossom laugh
and else forgotten – all of me lies in wait
to blind you passing where my blood was spilt
in oh my earthly my deliberate
white bird. And can you bear the guilt?'

FACES

Here their attack will come. Behind,
the vast home, anxious, close-frontiered;
the dim-lit scurry of the mind,
one's own land, ill-known, ware for war,
and amorous of what is feared.
A groping darkness lies before
– enemy country; and yet less
hostile than quite unknown, a guess
at speech and weapon, a no-more-
my-world, a shifting otherness.

And the attack will come between
– here, on this tender salient,
this almost-island only seen
(by garrison or foreign spy)
in unforeseeable event.
Close the bright calyx of the eye,
silence the coloured mouth, undress
the line of ordered comeliness:
here the invading flags will fly,
the sentry fall, and none possess
a lamp to tell his nation by.

STREET PERFORMERS, 1851

Street performers...admit of being classified into:
(a) mountebanks – or those who enact puppet-shows, as Punch and Judy, the fantoccini, and the Chinese shades...
(b) the street-performers of feats of strength and dexterity, as...stiff and bending tumblers, salamanders, swordsmen, etc...
(c) The street-performers with trained animals – as sapient pigs, dancing bears, and tame camels.

(Henry Mayhew: *London Labour and the London Poor,* 1851)

London is painted round them: burly railings
and grey rich inaccessible houses; squares –
laurelled and priveted, flowered, and fast in palings –
where the grave children move and are not theirs
and are more bright and distant than the sun
whose wan dry wine shines in the windows – squares
and heavy curtains, curtains and steps of stone:
these are their coloured cards, their theatres.

Hooked nose and hump, the Black Man, the police,
the hangman's shadow by the prison wall,
the wandering misery in the courts of peace:
the mad voice like a wire will draw them all –
the puppets and the puppet-masters. Watch:
who is to tell, seeing no showmen's heads,
which are the audience, penny-foolish, which
the fantoccini and the Chinese shades?

Now (scarlet plush and gilt) the lights go on;
cold smoky curtains fold the stage away;
and all but shadows, penny plain, are gone.
Flare-cast from vehement oil, great blurs of grey
upon the gold and indigo, their dole
habit's iniquity and ungiven bread,
they drift before the rainy street; they roll
on sad wheels rags to be inherited.

The salamander and the swordsman, and
the maypole-ribboned bear: from dark they pass
to dark, through blazing islands – as if stained
in mockery upon hot slips of glass.
And the flame dies; the fingers are withdrawn;
the puppets tumble; there are no more slides;
the paints are in their boxes: they have gone,
the fantoccini and the Chinese shades.

A HYMN FOR EVE

Here in his garden, water flows
bright as a stream of birds, the brown
and jewel-glitter of birds' eyes,
the grain of eyes; and here the sun,
bee-gold and swarming, murmurs on
a grass as ripe as flesh. The soil
is coarse and fragrant, and the rocks
are heavy flowers. Here how cool
and soft the fruits; how warm the cheeks –
a seraph walking shadowless –
the gentle air will press to mine.
            And he who made my nakedness
a song of living warmth, my skin
fragile as windflower silver, made
my strength of body suave and white,
for Adam's and his own delight,
he gave me liberty of pride
as if in garden, beast, or fruit,
because all beauty must be his.
Yet I am clothed as no beast is:
for, as the sun-chord wraps the mote,
my lords enfold me in their voice
and swathe me in their gale of light.
Nor have I need but I may bind
the garden round me for my dress:
the river's freshly-sliding coat
spangles my body; or the wind
faint as the breathing of this hand
not on my breast but near and warm,
weaves tissue such as angels own.
Pelted with gold, by day I wear
on breast and eye and every limb
the smooth stiff texture of the sun;
and in my tired his darker time,

lest even pebbles should lie bare,
in softer beauty shades are spun
from violet branch and grey-gold air.
            This world that I am in is good:
orders of touches lights and stones
and reasons by themselves are food.

And I have wise companions.

A HYMN FOR ADAM

Sun of amazement, manifold
as the grey flush of wind in grass,
as all your angel-moons, as cold
of star-thought of star-fluted space:
all times and all directions bend
inward upon themselves at last;
for they have met you at their end
and have no roads for going past.

The glacier's gathered muscle, furred
with souls of breathless music, still
breaks the unripple of your word
and loosens tongues towards your will.
For the unchanging is your dance;
infinite speed is motionless;
your power is quiet circumstance
and silence is your blessedness.

Yet you have spoken to our flesh
because we closed the inward ear,
because we struggled in the mesh
of eyeless evil and its fear:
and leaning down like a gold wind
to feel the moments of the flood,
you hear the sunlight, see behind
the warmth we carry on our blood.

Between the cortex and the twig
your eyes have seen your heralds pass;
the virgin belly of the fig
has closed upon your resting place:
you who conceived along your voice,
you who are infinite and small,
did not compel our needless choice,
will not let fallen children fall.

You who are knowledge, gave us earth
to be our servant, and had care
to build the planets round our birth:
will you send more than we can bear?
In murderous throat and raging eyes
and in the leaping talon, still
you have preceded us; there lies
the peace of your unmoving will.

LILITH

If he had been contented with the apple
I hardened for him from the water-shadow;
or known the beasts by my names; or be able
to thread my glamour through the guarded meadow;
if, happy in the rib and single hair
I dressed for him in sweat and he thought woman,
he had not seen or heard the shining air
speak to him; or believed my mirror-demon,
I who am daughter of the glass of God;
or if he had lain still with witchcraft, ridden
the centaur-spider of his enchanted blood
– how could he lose, or want, or know, an Eden?

Angels unsheathed him; Eden drove me out,
binding itself my absence in his love.
Which are the real garden and the doubt?
How can he tell my image from my grave?
He will search after me in his own heart,
and find me, and not know if I am Eve.

THREE CHRISTMAS TREES

The tree of night has all its candles lit,
and dreams are piled about its foot: oh son,
oh sleeping son, what do you take from it?
There is no age in sleep; the boy is one
with infant and with patriarch: how guess
what shining branches lift, or rivers run,
on what far day, in this your timelessness?

Are you companion to that other boy
whose parents' dreams lay round him as he slept?
Between them in their sleep, what starry joy
of leaves arose, what holy river crept
– Jordan, the olives green round Galilee?
Or innocent blood, and tears that Rachel wept;
an only gift upon a fatal tree?

Son, do not wake too early. All tonight
is yours to bid, a safe deceiver; day
with all its presents opened, every light
its coloured mystery lost, will not obey.
Late rising to your Paradise, take all
our other gifts; but let the apple stay
on that tree's bough, which breaking, you will fall.

THE SWORDS OF GLASS

I turn in the morning to defy, as I pass
the shabby antique-shop window, the swords of glass:
a blue crossing a green, but on each hilt
a bine of crimson, a frozen braid of gilt
and of water-crystal. Their twin smooth tips are sharp
as briars; the blades though flute and twist and warp
like barley-sugar if it glittered, or the gold
shafts of a roundabout. Self-enclosed and cold,
they creep with childhood's nausea for the too
richly-confected plane that is not quite true.
As these are not: not toys, yet they would smash
to sharp confetti round the fighter; never a flash
in beauty or gallantry; they have never been
crossed, but in mocking rest, the blue and the green.

I know them, the nature of all glass, the old sly
shallowness of the goat's, the parrot's and the Arab's eye:
the blind perspective sparkle. Glass is a liar:
the air of images, witch-water, the dead man's fire;
dark-diamonded room of earth, light without heat,
where dazzle of limbeck and hell of mirror meet.
Lies, they have stabbed at lies, and the gesture lied.
The blue sword entered drily a dust-bubble's side,
dust in damnation's effigy of a Christ; and there
an evil Nothing vainly crucified air.
Strong in the green sword, Satan leaned above a well,
stabbed his own image, flared like a nova, and fell.
Colours and acts met on the mirror's face:
hell's ingrown icicle, suicide of glass,
I turn in the morning to defy as I pass.

THE FOOL IN 'LEAR'

Mad as a bee or a wild shining bird,
my only genus is to mock:
I am the sad wasp, and the robin sick
with dancing in the cold; I am the word
that opens, in your dreams, the hideous door;
I am the sex of weather; strip me bare,
I am the laughing stock.

Down in the horrible mystery, the night
and granite of the old king's mind,
the grief and writhing cracked across; went blind
and venomous: it was thence that I crept out.
Which of us, in his madness, was the man?
Only my knowledge went to bed at noon,
his was the staring wind,

his was the bed in which I left no trace:
nothing could prove I had been born;
I had gone back. Yet sometimes he had worn
wrinkles or troubled hair that were my face;
dying himself, it was in me he wrapped
Cordelia, one hour before I slipped
into the cold again.

BROMPTON CEMETERY

I

White in the anguish of their desolate acres,
the yardstones of the dead
shine on the land like everlasting breakers;
and the sunlight flickers
over the willow of the angel's head
to the tin wreaths and the gilding
and the sad memory of flowers enfolding
bone and bronze and bed.

Over the natural dust of man's dishonour,
small calvaries of the grave,
angel and crucifix mourned alike with mourner
later or sooner
hang towards darkness like a powerless wave.
Living and faith and hoping:
empty, deferred, and crowned with thorns of weeping,
themselves they cannot save.

Six feet dark in the earth's organ-breathing,
all waves abate:
glory and lack and the cut grin of loathing
lie down and wait for nothing,
and grow so small they do not know they wait.
Sudden and long is the mourning
for the prodigal of love returning:
he returns too late.

II

Gold hearts of sunlight on the Thames
repeat the stone and filigree,
keep Gaudy for their death in flames
the many-backed and blazing sea;
gardens of silences bequeath

their coloured carillons to the air:
and summer is a painted wreath
above an infinite despair.

Dance heart and flower while you may;
the earth you spread gallanted once:
much has been paid and is to pay
for generations of the dance.
A garden is a widowed grief
and every grief a vase of bells
and every bell a human life
and every life a wave that falls.

III

When funeral ink is faded; when
grief comes like bills; and when the brave
imperfect flesh, its beauty gone,
grows dry and little in the grave:
Will one pathetic bone beneath
its dumb and windless cloak of lead
believe that death is always death,
and know the pity of the dead?

What leman in your linen form
will shiver at the hunter's foot?
What lover's hollow in the arm
be full again where you are not?
The thoughts you thought eternal, and
your bodies' endless reckless need,
are a scar in wasted ground,
and know the pity of the dead.

Because we set our joy behind
a bastion of delights and vows,
now there are days of naked wind
and comfort failing in no house.

The common smile, the ticking phrase
so often sad so often said,
sign you like portraits: leave us these,
and know the pity of the dead.

INVOCATION UPON THE DEATHS OF GREAT MEN

Their day was eloquent: morning was the spun
blue savagery of wind, and noon the call
of trumpeters to lions. Triumph undone,
warm in the ebb of bee-light was begun
their dying: colour of autumn; the grey scrawl
of ash-of-apricot upon the wall,
that names us weighed and finds us wanting. *Seal*
their sunlight on our dark, you who appal
our closing landscape – moon, their mirror of steel,
oh face of Lazarus, look down and heal.

They died among their jewelled evening: none
to hear their anger, feel or hear at all
the honey and lions'-mating of their sun
grow sour and impotent. But one by one
the alien lesser stars dare and grow tall –
night's peacock, light of the gnat's voice. *In our hall*
of kneeling shadows, give us grace to kneel
self-shadowed. Angel or eagle or animal,
moon, from the wasting of your cherub wheel,
oh face of Lazarus, look down and heal.

Not in this nightyear may their cataract stun
with honey of wrath of thunder and carnival
by golden milk. But we, the million
trillings of little silver, glitter and run
and whimper through the dark: we are the small
vibrations of dead music, we must crawl
through strings we cannot sound. *You who repeal*
the deaths of suns – you their memorial –
even such waking Lemures you anele:
oh face of Lazarus, look down and heal.

Fierce blazon upon earth, armorial
colours we cannot fire – we stoop and reel
under the sea-weight of their weapons; fall
by theft of honour. *Moon whose moons we steal –*
oh face of Lazarus – look down and heal.

SCIENCE FICTION

Death is by burning, on this planet; burning
alive before it is too late; and birth
is common, towards the end – there is no mourning,
for there is no cold interval: first breath
and last, being ardent and vermilion,
flowering and falling in voluntary ash,
are like an heirloom, like the heirloom sun:
he is Their god; They eat his fiery flesh.

But he is not my sun – a different colour,
and vast and bad. And shall such things be done
where Liberty brings Progress and The Dollar?
I shout, and reach for my atomic gun.
Besides, They have too odd a shape to live;
a complex language; no respect. And creatures
who look at everything we want to give,
and look away, must have disloyal natures.

They have no passions: full freshwater seas,
and mauve and orange fields; caverns and woods
upon the spiring mountains – among these
Their meetings are angelic solitudes,
Their only food the wisdom and the fire;
dead-petalled light Their shelter and Their clothing.
The wisdom is the fire: star-Eden where
infinite apples burn on boughs of Nothing.

Why do my fingers freeze upon the blaster
as if (not I, for I am loyal) They
rebelled by wonder? May we not die faster,
dying by dark and cold, than those we slay?
But I am still a man: They have no rockets,
no private counterprise; They think and need
nothing that comes in small transparent packets:
kill Them, kill all Their foul inhuman breed!

TRIPTYCH

Whom at the first we kill
(angel that bears us truth
immediate and ill;
hound of the warning tooth):
lay truths as towered walls,
bite like the warden beaver:
in our unpictured cells
guard us for ever.

Whom in the end we keep
(ikons of Self and Why
and You; the names of hope
named indefensibly):
people our small belief,
our dusk of single vision:
to us a mask for grief;
to you unreason.

Whom all the time we are
(shells of the unborn child,
the uncaged ancestor;
paths in a poisoned field):
through neither wall nor mask
let us observe and pity:
our neighbour in the dusk,
our frightened city.

CASE HISTORIES

I
SUMMER IDYLL
The Arcadian Poets

Here on the dunes, where children's pumping feet press home
into the tawny breasts, and rattle
the fallen bones of cliffs (before, the gleam
of a great emerald-glass crawling petal;
behind, the bungalows as trim and bright with paint
as little yachts) I lie; and if I look,
the grass against them circles me, sharp and intent
and stiff as rigging; shadows of gulls wave back.

Here in the velvet lion's-paws of sun, the purr
of sleepy light, I rest; and hear the summer
wheel round me like my blood; and watch the fire
– garnet, black and gold – feel the murmur
of heat upon my lids: earth dances now; and heat,
reeling in the bruised pebbles round me, stares
like an audience through her shining garments, her light
melismata of lacy skirt of flowers.

In such a time, the heart erect with happiness,
what else to think but the cool apple-blossom
flush of an early love? – how else caress
myself upon the moment's lissom
its flesh-warmed silk; feel quivering beneath my hand
live articulations, commerce of skin,
a lover's body pleased and flowering out of sand?
And revisiting love haunted by the sun?

Love naked among boughs and garlands, among
the feather-growing cold of woods, and flushed
with coral under honey; love with a tongue
of birds and fountains, where birds and fountains flashed
like a bowl of jewels; love simple as a hand;
legend or pastoral: kinder than the sweet
aching of Amaryllis, than the sound
(through gilded groves and fields) of Daphnis' flute:

not only gods were sure of it. For mortals,
bright from the running and the flower-throwing,
soft hands of air lascivious in their kirtles
– love on the tasselled grass where spring was strewing
the excellently shining pools of sheep,
stood round them strong and innocent as the sun:
bodies awake as burning eyes, all else asleep:
the love, the lovers, and the place, were one.

She, if immortal, dancing like a sunny field,
the grass of Paradise, and poets there;
a gentle house, unguarded as a child,
wide as the splendour of the air.
Mortal, then rooted in what innocence, to be
the grace and perfume of a tree,
sweet as a lilac walking? – and her words
like jewels dropping into water, all her speech
delicate as an eyelash or her touch;
and fingers like the bones of little birds.

So, like a yacht's abandonment of all self
but the grace only, a strong and comely sail,
they leaned on loving. Summer: the restless gulf,
the walking in us of a masterless will:
veins running sunlight, the body one fierce hand
of agony of love. And water beat,
drowning in brilliance, gently by us, to the sound
(through gilded groves and fields) of Daphnis' flute.

Tree after tree alive in leopard's clothing
swung into curtains, and bowed us into shade
under whose lace of leaves the softly breathing
grass beckoned round us; and smooth and free and wide
as doors, the wind was opened upon day.
Oh calmly rocking sky, and the sun a fall
of angels shouting over us; love, the land at play
– the reeling land where birds were bountiful
and love a star in the heart, and love in the mouth
like strawberries, and the amazed flesh sensitive as a moth.

For such an amorous Arcadian space of air,
of mother-kindly air more gently turning
than a warm infant's head, more smooth and near
than a wife's cheek; its huge blue burning
intimate as a bed – for such a cone and pulse
of spangled wind, the self unfolds as for
a bride; its memory trails fingers through her pearls;
the figment and the truth rise and mean war.

Tired of the tireless rocking in a million beds,
all birth behind her, careless now of praise,
like an old woman, the sea smiles and nods;
the sunlight aching in her eyes.
Lips that were once Cassandra's or the leap of wolves,
now ineffectual as eyelids, fall
and fold and writhe and fall and lisp over themselves
and their soft food, the shore's most glittering scroll.

II
AUTUMN PASTORAL
The Metaphysicals

Now as the declining sun
makes a wide autumn in the water that all day
lifted the glittering music of its leaves, and they
whisper their delicate frost upon
a shore grown old with its desertions; now
all that lives by season takes its noon
about it like a cloak – our hearts must know,
breaking upon their boundaries, their season too.

Oh love, love that comforts like a bed
but blindly, in the misted flesh, knows of its loss,
loving aware but not awake: the sad
wondering of the ape's and the dog's face –
those blunted images of spring – is all its good.
Now, in the flush
of wincing red and gold that lies
lovely upon the fountains and the barren waves,
the mystery of branching flesh
– trees' tawny breasts, and coloured commerce of the leaves
beautifully awake as eyes:
in eyeless love, the touch and ecstasy of surfaces,
light in the lost water, in the tall
magniloquence of burning boughs, ended their will.

Oh need, the echo in the trembling grove;
the Greensleeves habit wherein lovers tired;
the virgin like a mirror watching love
too soon possessed: for what Elizabethan lord,
whose mated passion held in check by tears
was but a queen in pawn to be advanced,
was chastity worn? were there no other gears
to dress the fallen? Bodies that glanced

like fever and October through the heart
laid hands of medicine on the season's hurt.

What would they have then? Love as bed and sacrifice,
the beast in angel air, and the sun stalking
guilty in the fields: convent of thought
and incest of emotions – to forget
in having all that urges to possess
and shame in breaking.
What loneliness came down upon them, shut
like autumn and a door, their dying light?

Rich in the bearded field the ripe
and panic-fluttering wheat is gathered: what can it gather
beyond the shudder of the act, strength torn together,
the now of children? or the shape
of bodies wise in bodies, sickle-flash
repeated to a mist, a death in motion, deep
glamour of silver on the rustling flesh?

They rose from a boy's dreaming, from a faceless act
anonymous and inhuman as the armoured sky:
a ceremony of disguise, a locked
and glassy gallery that watched them die
strong and pathetic as the animal
– rock under flinty sunlight, or the cast
on athletes' limbs of blonde imperious oil:
shallow appeasement of the artesian beast.

Else a great Prince in prison lies: oh Christ
were he alone; oh sharp intensity of bars.
Feeling the close and clamour of the doors,
pain like a runner's breast,
and vain hands upon them, and the floors
that did not echo to her feet (for dust,
dropping like evening from the deciduous room,

will settle everywhere softly at last),
I fed on portraits in the empty portraits' home.

I ate the stubble of love, echo of grain:
bleak interlunar interseason of male thought,
with a rod of blood between us. Sometimes when
the windy curtains like a landscape shut
our separate rising into pain,
remembering that rod of blood, we knew
ourselves left naked in the rut of passion
to watch the feeble writhing wave that grew
(till we became each other's superstition)
in thundery space the desolation of wind,
dark mansions of unfaithfulness.
The love that grew among the foreign leaves,
the spoiled thing, is powerful: it lives:
and we were stained and parted by its guilty glass.

Error by burning; grief of the wave too weak
for the dry pebble; debt of the running bird:
and every error, every falling-back,
hurt like the sound of doors, was hard
as peaches bitten to the naked bone,
or the axe in the oak.
For through the lovely clothing of their myth
danger wore outward, was revolt or death,
was loving better what they chose to lack.

The shining flocks darkened upon the field;
legend or pastoral slept like jewels in
a world of ceremony unfulfilled:
love being torn and vexed by sin
by insufficiency by thought, being laid
a barrier like sad music played
between desire and will: between the hunger
and the quivering plenty: lion or light of anger,

but always lonely as an eye, always afraid,
the false intangible fencing of a love's convention:
dark forest, and dark mansion.

Here is the spacious pity of
the evening, grey medicinal-smelling woods grow cold
about me; black with sunset the adored boughs hold
their thin bright hands above
landscape and sky, the fire and echo of bronze.
The air is like a bather's flesh: and grave
with odour of dying; with the sound of bones
dropped underfoot in drifts, frailer – and dry – than veins.

Sadness like orphans: but I choose
the waste uncertainty and splendour of this calm:
not the autumnal organ-throat, imperial time
flushed thick with velvet suns that bruise
the orchards under sweetness; not the torn
virginity of woman-scented corn,
the honeyed pearl and languor of her loosened thighs.

There in the drumming rush and weight,
the lechery, the sweet-juice-ecstatic hours
that swarmed with the cathedral majesty of emperors
drunk under swinging ponderous light,
our blood was hurled within us like a ball
poised one perpetual second after flight:
shudder of drowning in the thirsty pool,
moment of birds that fall
unalterably through the printed gale of wheat.

I choose what love became, this troubled season.
Only our bodies being separate remember
fields in their summer of quick early amber
or, through the spare and breathy glass of this horizon,
themselves a cornucopia. Between

the sun and this our sunless lilac-pouring green,
the tremor and the reaping have grown cold as prison;
a lack in love with pain.

In cages of dark air the rooks,
wrestling their palisades like the shadows of gulls,
feel the year tremble: heart of enormous dying bells:
the wind where all the landscape shakes
to a leashed yacht: feel the year tremble. The eye
knows that whenever year comes back or makes
this absence whole, it must be hard and shy –
winter, a watching, and like tolerance of a lie.
Only the sun, the season, the heart, know,
breaking upon their boundaries, their season too.

III
WINTER ELEGY
The Shakespearian Tragic Heroes

The room is cold: night moves in it
like hands, the commerce of dead flesh; I stand alone
and feel the season's lips, silence of star and moon,
the mineral bitter silence, eat
as rat or pox eats, round me – diamond
of cold, gnashed naked facet of the bone.
From this dark lantern I look out, on wind
leaping with huge paws horribly its dancing-ground.

This is the weather of the wolf's fur; this
is ikon-weather; pale cathedral cold
in frozen images. There where no room is,
no bed except the old
unsearching earth – oh flood,
oh organ-throat of the great modal wind, roaring
like summer suns, the black whips whistling, the devouring
saltsea moonlight fingering the blood!
And the sad shining of the armour, bearing
my father, bearing my years away, bearing my God.

Cold like a gnat's voice, a taut wire;
cold singing like an edge: and in it, anger
shudder and bugle, clangour
of power in fabric, strangling of strength, sleet
hissing like hatred at the mothering fires;
and fire of darkness burning on the winter's feet
in a fierce wide-open falling of kingdoms – where
only the ghost moves, or the enemy stars.

We walk tonight: and ikon-armour shines,
rags gutter, in the candles of the snow;
ravaged boughs and curtains beat their chains

on madness rising like a menacing bird:
oh let me not be mad… what evil now
flowers out of memory to the drumming word
remember? – and foreboding being all I know?
What beast roars to this landscape that I read
for the earth's answer: 'This is room, and bed, and you'?

I know I have grown old: this evil place
so old the former lineaments of land
rise through it: it is thus my loosening face
wears down to bear my ancestors: to end.
Storm: and I hear within me chattering ghosts
of No and Then and Now: and they are I
returning, many as a wood, to die.
I have become my history, my many pasts.

And surely after me no future? Surely
the bodies I had learnt like music, the desires
of kind and form, deeper than root or blood, the fears
– all we exchanged so tenderly and early,
like rings – die with me? And what in age,
beyond the blizzard of my years, oh still
I turn: the child's face, the for-ever-blemished page
never to turn, weeping, never to change and all be well?

Oh inaccessible as time (haunter
of your betrayals the usurped heart) waif of my horror,
crier at windows, never to grow or live or enter,
white face like a wave: oh mirror:
am I not Love as you were? so
love to Love, the flashing gust to crow
and seven-fiery crystal in the candelabrum air,
over their pain's uncovered page, the eyes laid bare;
over the moonlit violet-shining foam of snow.

For what have I to see but, rack and wheel,
still time? And time grown inward like a tooth – lust
and a simian rage, cut grinning throat of disgust
and pity? In their own devouring gale,
lost haters and lost lovers – fire on icy fire,
around them blazes the last ache of ill,
the fierce wide-open falling of angels; where
passionless as altars burn the cold of hell
and – for we walk tonight – an enemy star.

For what have I to see but lovers bearing
one thick-whispering image a hot hand on the eyes?
The sleeplessness of hurt when the flesh lies
drowned as a drugged man: image image image staring
like a wild drumming burning under unturning skies:
the image: heavier than statues, sick
as dark blood, cut veins' transfusion of the dark:
image of alien lust. Have they not felt
(lost lovers and lost haters) the vertigo-printed
hollow in sweet grass or in sand, the scented
oil of love's handling on the breast, the spilt
light of love patterned over act and limb?
And love like slime
in the mouth, a second mouthing of the cold spat meat
of strangers; like a crumpled garment come
hot from a hated body – and its shape and sweat
pulling the skin like leeches? *It*
is the cause, my soul … the writhe and clutch and hurt
and image image image of the cause, and noise
of the coiled cause loud as the suckling of the seas.

And yet it was not Love that made
an aching season round them, echo and path
of one wide autumn poured into the bed:
but that oh sharp oh that irrevocable death
when two can never be alone again, but vainly

masked in conspiring silence, masked and lonely.
Therefore not Love, but field and aftermath
– the trembling company of mown waves – that never
can be alone and flowering for a waking lover:
straws that sleep strangled under the madman's breath.

Out of the knife and prison of embracing
slip the pale captives; from that loosening womb
a bastard envy, treachery's unloosing.
That mated passion should beget this flame!
All they could not be, desired, nor may,
the dagger's oily tooth, the inward scream
of the live bolt thrust home:
there is the stranger crouching to his play;
death in the shadow of the crown;
and the great wind shouting my kingdom down.

Oh tightening springes, snow upon fire of blood,
the world's wind naked on the skeleton, the white
ruin of stars behind betrayed eyes; red
image image image roaring in its horrible bed.
Oh sprung cogs' intolerable fire,
turned with the turning motion of the heart,
crookedly wrenching, spoiling, weaving fear:
still in the beauty of all this burning height
I see the appalling legend of desire,
and the hurt creature twisting in the night.

It needs no ghost… tomorrow and tomorrow… and
from war and stabbing arras, oh what birth
so long remembered under armour breaks upon
the steely ringing bitten impotence of earth?
Or ripens from the blue reverberant stone
of our torn seasons, a live and amorous fruit,
a double body pleased and flowering from the death
of king and chaos, withering sun and root?

A bitter heaven like a scattered hearth,
mad in the age and anger of sceptres, lies
empty: the turning of their scornful eyes,
the living mineral net of stars;
the gods forsaking us behind
betrayal, the vulcanic ambush of adulteries
where Venus melts the visored lip of Mars
and the fierce mesh of wind
circles with huge coils horribly their dancing-ground.

Lying alone, inhabited with all my past,
the world a closed and singing claw of steel,
I hear the voices of the imagined dead,
they who were born for winter. Room and bed
ring the armour and the cry of the ghost,
the full ripe circling of the wheel.
This to my bitten pillow... This is my school;
this to the fingers of the cold and broadening waste.

RESOLUTIONS OF A COMMITTEE

...next, we resolve to use no more, except as a plaything,
any poetic mask or vestment; never to stand
before footlights – and least in grief or love, since nothing
is worth much weeping-for, unless perhaps everything; and
few things worth praising but those we insult by praise.
Though ritual mask and robe are worn by the magician
in his blood-painted zodiac, summoned power obeys
only the blood itself – the blood and the ambition:
we choose the other and the living, organ or flower,
in truth of self, to conjure-with (never the pleated
cloth of sham poppies, not the tin dancer, nor the sweet-sour
breath of old vases, or old satins, long vacated).

Therefore: resolved that knowing is to be undressed; and then
the naked mystery under the familiar garment
be caged in words, for singing; and the garrulous pen
be made a needle, to record it without comment.
Let all observations marry the daughters of music,
and reason take the colours of the colibri:
wise rainbows in the perspex of a metaphysic,
to shine and sing between planets, or in the sea.
For only the Aurora is the air of magic,
and only magic the proper body of intellect:
all else unmakes the poem, bridebed of wonder and logic,
the childing double splendour of prism and star-elect.

Resolved moreover that we the resolvers, we alone,
bear the gold wands of makars, the white swords of critics:
we pick no quarrel with incantation, with wit, with bone-
lipped thesis, or with madness, or with mathematics;
though we dislike, we scorn to condemn, the man
who faces carious ruin with continual stucco:
for we contain all failures; we are their sum, which can
forgive its tinted fossil or its quavering echo.

But we resolve – and this is our last resolution
as poets with one voice – that the committee adjourn,
singly, to virginal wrestling for its own possession
of the lunar nine-quetzal-clad Muses, and their return.

THE PLANETS

And this the Sonne is overal
The chief Planete imperial,
Above him and benethe him thre:
And thus between hem regneth he.
(John Gower: *Confessio Amantis,* vii, 865 – 8)

Under the rings and green of syrup-water
the great pond-fish in pewter, darkly weaving,
flutter their waving twilight. But to the watcher
warm in another nature, living the sun,
no creature, none, stirs in those coiled abysses;
and where those feathered nooses run, no dreamer
guesses the man, the summer, or his maker.

Now lean above and play the manna-maker:
here where the willows chequer the skylit water,
scatter your bread. The lurker and the dreamer
loom their cold glitter to the warmer sun:
swimmer by swimmer, one by one, come weaving
up from the laving of their spun abysses –
great heaving fish lift faces towards the watcher.

Fierce in appalling blue there stands the Watcher,
fire of our nurture, shining-weather-maker,
walker in awful stature of abysses.
All those pale gases' weaker light the Sun
disperses with his own, as his the water:
those outer mysteries burn, invisibly weaving,
brighter by his removing from the dreamer.

Sunless infinity will drown the dreamer
though, by the glimmer of the stars, the watcher
nightly – the stitcher of that dimmer weaving,
by night believing in a future sun –
calls it the crown of loving of our Maker:

darker than fish in their strange town of water,
day-bitter stars flicker in blind abysses.

Out of the poet's pardons and abysses
the verses rise like fish; around the dreamer
the glamour of wild spaces rolls like water:
fact will not flatter – the armour of the sun
breaks down; there is no quarter for the watcher.
Though richer by his wane, with sun the makar
– searcher of meeker stars – heddles their weaving.

Poems and stars and fish, all darkly weaving,
sieving the mystery of their proud abysses,
go roving – secret races – till the makar
undresses, for the waker in the sun,
beauties that shun the talker and the dreamer:
the lying moon is for the rhymer, the watcher
of selves that shimmer on a pitcher of water.

For mystery is the poem's night and water:
daughter of truth, clad in the spectral weaving
of her begetter our cold-earth-wiving Watcher,
she – marcher about that unforgiving Sun
whose archer-beams we enthrone in wheeled abysses –
wears unknown light's embraces, until the dreamer
ceases to murmur against stars or Maker.

NOTES FOR A MYTH
(1968)

PART ONE
SYMBOL AND MYTH:
AN HOUR-BOOK FOR LOVERS

THE BELLCOTE

Lean on the ropes; you need not ask
how many will swing dumb, nor care
such limping courses are a task
not for the arm but for the air.
An iron fist that clubs a shell
of iron on the lips, may tongue
with no more music than a bell
cast memberless or never rung.
But let the poems hope to speak
though impotent or cracked and sour
(or draught and rust their only sound).
The willing ear is not so weak:
it knows of tigers in the tower
that roar the homing changes round.

IMAGES IN A DUSTBOWL

Catching the corner diamonds, where
both images break white,
couples will stare at bonds
that seem harmonious light.

Quicksilver clouds their faces; yet
"All I would have you see
(in the forgetting glasses)
were love lent them by me.

"The lying-brawl deceives us, bends
to desert or to waste
those who will end by leaving
a maze impurely paced.

"Honour and flesh are valent, though
their crops be lame and quelled,
such winds as blow are violent,
and the trees have been felled".

Mere worship ends in a mirror; lust
in drought and vigilance.
How much dust and error
before Love learns to dance?

A VILLANELLE IN MAY

Oh listen to no voice but mine,
your flesh be strung for only me,
and let us dance our own design.

Love and the dance are serpentine;
but when we kiss beneath the Tree,
oh listen to no voice but mine.

The ribbons flash and intertwine
to set our lifted sapling free
and let us dance our own design
across the alien pipe and shine
of covens' belled and mirrored glee:

oh listen to no voice but mine,
though dalliance and the sun combine
to coupled music: let them be,
and let us dance our own design.

And when the coloured airs decline
and the bright morris changes key,
oh listen to no voice but mine,
and let us dance our own design.

NOTES TO AN EPISTLE

(1 John iv. 7, 18)

Their barriers fell to a bolt of brightness,
and the flood swelled, found them, and carried them far:
love, more lucid and lambent around them
than the wind soaring, wheat-scented,
or the sun's greeting, golden-angeled,
by the broad molten gate of the blue:
love unlooked-for, a lordly spring
winging to the wilderness, shy-flowered.

The eyes not innocent, nor hands idle;
the flesh kindling like a butterfly unfolded;
meshed hair honey to the hungry scent,
a darling net dared by the diving fingers;
sweetness of skin, warmth-of-water-sliding;
mouths mortised in one, like music:
beauty of body under touch or breath;
and fire thrilling through the fruit of his thighs.

Fear shall not walk in the four ways
wedded here: the hearts in their high pasture
of cherishing, of charity, of chosen rest:
and sensual bodies in the sweetness of sparing,
meeting as by magnets although unmated.
Fear shall not follow nor freight their love
guilt geld it nor debase its gold;
nor barriers, broken, rebuild against it ever.

THE INTERPRETERS

And so he gave her flowers, whose five tongues,
and suave inhuman lips that drink the sun,
might speak to other senses than his own,
as with cold flame, silk that breathes, coloured wings.
Leeching survival from an alien
element, they would know such languages
as cured the strangeness between hers and his.

Strangeness, because all beauty and all love
walk the unusual ways, and are unsure
except of self and image: what is there
but crying-out to one-another *Give*
and, pleading, *Take?* The union, the pure
not-spoken marriage, needs interpreters
to cure the strangeness between his and hers.

And so he gave her flowers: yes, they died
almost at once. But, flower-sexed, and vased
in what they lived-by, these two lovers used
those emblems for the life of what they did:
no lovers learn the assurance of the dead,
but gift and symbol cannot die; it is
their commerce that keeps age from hers and his.

PROTHALAMION

Light – low far-clouded light, pale-flooding tide
of clarity and space – rise higher; break
the sea-wall of his rest; let him awake
                    and smile, as at the bride
whom you will bear to him. And for her sake
pour out your tenderness and all your power
and make them his. Be risen, virgin sky
of his last solitude, and lift on high
his wonder and his love, that from this hour
                    another world may flower.

World – you that have been, you that will be, hers –
do not arouse her yet; this is the grey
and indigo of morning, not of day.
                    No chorus, no cloud, stirs.
You then that sweep the dying world away,
forbid awhile the saffron streamers and
fierce hymeneal torches of your east:
she will have time for all when you have ceased.
Both worlds be gentle, and now most: command
                    your spinning hours to stand.

Sun, they will not. But sun that on my panes
coldly by callous glistening disobeyed,
leave her asleep awhile where she is laid
                    among your subtle chains:
all you see there is soon to be unmade.
Still in the calm and secret of her room,
as in a garden, wake the folded scents:
apple and flower and grass; the sweet warm tents
of her young bed; the petalled flesh in bloom
                    which is its own perfume.

Day, make her window glad; and when your blue
is a tall purity of splendour, lift
her unreluctant eyelids to that gift,
                and let her come to you.
Let her uprising and her blood be swift;
and when she greets you, wing your melting air
with strength to carry – oh invisible dove –
myrtle and rose between her and her love.
But let the voices of all those who bear
                love towards her, whisper there.

Air, dulcet air who were their messenger,
now let their separate innocence unite
because you kiss them both. Or shape the bright
                leagues that encircle her,
and shut him from her, to a weir of light –
a lens between them, by whose glittering bands
they are drawn close. Or make the burning-glass
from their own bodies, that the fire may pass
more keenly the wide focus of their hands
                than where her mirror stands.

Glass, happy glass, that to your lucid heart
may hold so much unhindered loveliness,
let all your coloured beams reach out and bless
                her body set apart,
which you may learn then all but one must guess.
This let her watch a little, while there stray –
remembering and prophetic, though her own –
hands on the moth's-wing of her flesh: long known,
but dedicate to strangeness by today,
                it has goodbyes to say.

Birds in your towers of sapphire, and that swim
gold-haunted reaches of the wind, and sing
down diamonds upon us: let the ring

that seals her now to him
be emblem of your jewelled ways, and bring
no thought less tender than our speech and yours.
But leave the purer circles that shall bind
the pair, by flesh and by the unchanging mind,
for songs of that flame-lilied host which soars
above your sunlit shores.

Hours, last ambiguous hours, too many though
too swift; way-builders whose high task it is
to arch above them sounds and images
by whose prismatic bow
her gentleness may join at last with his:
let every pace along your wheeling height
peal in their hearts and fill the world with bells.
All the exalted ceremony foretells
be in your passing, till through grave delight
you lead them towards the night.

Heralds of night – you, green and amethyst,
and breathing coolness of the fallen sun;
windflower spectre of the moon – have done,
and let them keep their tryst:
let the dark hair of evening be spun
into a curtain for their quietude.
And you, sweet emblematic star, alone
lift up your fire to make their meeting known;
and you alone, calm planet, bright renewed,
have license to intrude.

Moon, let them breathe you for angelic air,
and grow transfigured in your power, possessed
as by a sacrament they had not guessed.
Darken her eyes and hair,
darken the roses upon mouth and breast,
but wake her skin with silver: and for him,

bathe his unfolded strength and ardency
in the live ichor of your floods, that he
may wield a body built in every limb
as if of seraphim.

Love, lifted flail of bodies, fire of wind
that roars through flesh grown sensitive as eyes;
oh headlong music of the blood that cries,
but trembles, to be twinned:
burn, winnow, swell, this harp-strung night. And rise,
you throne of Charity, the steady pole
of all the wheels of stars, rise now above
these two and the first rituals of their love;
loose in their flesh that singing flame the soul,
to make this moment whole.

Moment, irrevocable moment, bring
nothing that gladness may not quench: no fear
but his, for pity, no endurance dear
beyond the welcoming.
But let the glories of the Grail and Spear
shine through their flesh as through cathedral panes,
and every touch be jewels, every act
be angels, every joy or hurt contract
to the one double flower in whose veins
run paradisal rains.

Stars, in the cloister of your mineral fire
forever virgin, guard them both, and keep
the amazement of the morning from their sleep:
all wonder and desire
at last are yours awhile. And envy. Weep,
then, for yourselves; but scatter on these two –
my friend and sister, and her love – no less
than tears of amber wept for happiness.

Or be her bridal crown, made nightly new
in your own healing dew.

Time, work no evil on their peace: adore,
still-vailing your implacable eyes, this trance
in the white halls of worship; make your dance,
too swift for motion or
the fury of music, one sweet circumstance.
But let the dance endure: they could not bear
eternity in all its nakedness:
be then yourself its fluid saffron dress;
shiver its light with torches; let it wear
your armour everywhere.

Light, fair Light infinitely springing, grace
all hours and seasons of these lovers, grown
by passionate mercy deeper than their own
each other's dwelling-place:
within them shine, and on this bed, the throne
and altar of their flesh; there flower and run,
rich Fountain, always; brightness, petal-fold
of spreading glory, break of pulsing gold,
adorn them: till, slow-lifted endless one,
you rise, oh Unseen Sun.

'FROM WHENCE HIS MOTHER ROSE'
(Sedley)

Sea-glaze from the cliff summit, a motionless green
adoration of sun (sun that adored our love)
till the white lips' writhing and the rocks of their pain –
flower-lovely-false, marginal, seen from above.

Sea-trance from the bed of weeds and shells, the leached
compassionate light of sickrooms: kingdom, though,
of crab and squid and small cold rivers – arched
with franchise, yet, and burnscape, felt from below.

Do not, oh never, dive: what stays behind
is all you live-by; what you carry down
will struggle pitiless; vox humana wind
you fall through, lies: by sea or sun, you drown.

KEEPSAKES

The tree, whose tear this resin was,
is dust beyond recovering;
yet, as in golden locket-glass,
its fossil grief preserves to us
fragilities of bud or wing.

Velvet and vein and rib are dry,
yet they are whole and are a rose;
the lexicon where they must lie
(of a dead speech that would not die)
outwears – like them – a flower that grows.

Sidereal weeping drowns what grew
five-petalled on our almanac
our tree of proverbs: how construe
the mummy-leaves when I, or you,
shall close the amber and the book?

"IN A STRANGE LAND"

Si oblitus fuero tui... (Psalm 137)

Beside the streams of Babylon
they broke their zither-strings, and wept;
from his Icarian island, John
saw their new City, narcolept.
But not in tears, nor while we slept,
was our more jewelled Zion built,
before the sigils were undone,
before the vials had been spilt.

To dream in exile, to awake
unmade from an apocalypse,
may cause more subtle strings to break
than tremble under finger-tips:
set as a seal on heart and lips,
names for diaspora withhold
what memories and visions make
or rainbow, sardonyx, or gold.

If I forget thee...? We shall not,
until our last and coldest grief
is to remember we forgot –
shut broken windows on the thief,
or bathe too late the withered leaf.
O quanta qualia...? But for these,
our coronets are bergamot,
our palaces the willow-trees.

BALLADE OF NEW PROVERBS

For these the orange, and for those the rind;
starve on the stalk, or grow upon the grain;
the ripest walnut leaves a shell behind;
the crust of sweetness is the mourner's bane;
none eats the leaf on which the stone has lain;
we die by poisons of our own invention;
no idler to repent than to refrain;
there is no healing love by first intention.

War and the wilderness are strong to bind;
the softer flesh must learn the sharper chain;
the face of evil does not hurt the blind;
the naked man is not afraid of rain;
pity is water to remembered pain;
the power of cruelty rests in apprehension;
the wound of pleasure leaves the deepest stain;
there is no healing love by first intention.

The spying lover knows what he will find;
the trodden wheat goes last into the wain;
the careless torture is the most unkind;
only the fool has never need to feign;
the fisher in the dew baits hooks in vain;
we learn the pitfall by the circumvention;
the tree is timber, but the roots remain;
there is no healing love by first intention.

The mountain shadow makes a sorry plain;
grief is a text that suffers no recension;
the virgin milk is never drunk again;
there is no healing love by first intention.

A LETTER IN GREEN INK

Jelosie be hanged bi a cable!
(Chaucer: *The Complaint of Venus*)

The hinges turn like eyes, the bolts are oiled;
but I have heard the entries of them all
you kissed by glances and the guilt half-smiled
(I saw); wrote secretly (but I can read
through leather, teak or sleep); whom you would call
on other telephones (on ours at need,
when I was absent: I could eavesdrop, though,
on *your* voice if it whispered overseas);
met lyingly or secretly (but no:
I was the mousefoot at your side). All these
I have discerned: oh, little fool, I *knew*
even before my knowledge became true!

I am the chooser of the poisoned cup;
crooked with pain, researching after pain;
I am the weeping spy, the adder-up
of almost-nothings to a deathly sum –
in binaries, ah yes, and my not-sane
computer does not fear a minimum:
when it adds 1 and 1, it answers 10.
No barbarous impeachment, no sick act,
no labyrinth of plea, revolts me *then:*
I judge and sentence by unjuried fact.
But oh my God my darling my free dove,
can you not see my twisted strength is love?

NOTES FOR POP SONGS

I *Lock-out*
No shuttle in the secret mill
is moving; on his banished hill
the mole is crucified and still.

In the strait fevers of the bed,
truly wed or priestly wed,
care and its comforter are dead.

Left hand erases right's intent;
neither knows where this year went;
no season calendered but Lent.

Thought and finger dip too deep:
weep then alone, or dreaming weep,
when the only joy is sleep.

II *Voyage à Cythère*
The last hotel is closing,
the sun goes in for good;
rain on the empty beaches,
mould on the foreign food:
back to the gate and curtains,
the pub along the road.

She carries little with her
but currency of time:
write out the passport-poem
(why are your fingers numb?)
and launch her on her journey
to love, the long way home.

Aboard, lost now already,
soon for the misting seas
she stands; but not her shadow:
long on the quay it lies.
Kneel then to lay like pennies
your kisses on its eyes.

AFFLICTIONS OF METAL

Love, gentle mirror-lattice, forged in the sun, web-light,
silver of evening windows: keep the rain away,
          and the sour breath we move-in, keep from it
the sooting candles of the ordinary day.
Oh if you must, let it face inwards, even; for
          lupus and cancer of the metals may
soon fall on it, and you not watch it any more.

Schist or detritus of the metals: poison-green
for copper; scarlet minium the ash of lead;
          the grey and shivering plague that falls on tin;
iron that rots in coal-wings or in friable blood:
all their cosmetic ruins, paintbox leprosies,
          are the new-smelted elemental deed
which acid fear, church-fire, time's weeping, oxidise.

We roast our dirt to paint-with, mingle dulcet oil
with ash of earth or metal; and the colours leap
          in life to which the elements were dull.
Refuse then easy mourning; let our clay burn-up,
summer amazement rust, shame etch our innocence:
          when all are dead, their dust is ours to keep –
the autumnal palette of despair and tolerance.

A DREAM OF JUDGMENT

Dark of the long grey street (its end unseen);
mist-aureoled lamps, and rain like fuchsia-drops;
bricks like an eczema, sore stone, a mean
ill slype among gnawn tenements and shops.
Strangers unsheltered and unglancing; crawl
of the toad of wind; my lost limp towards the fog:
no movement else: two shall inherit all –
December and the power of the dog.

Some errand brought me, by some netted way.
Why did I leave you in a firelit room,
naked, and soon to know the crouching play
of one I could have hindered – and for whom?
I follow the street onwards (will it lead
into the next, and rescue?); but I find
walls at my face. Back the sad miles: no need,
and no flame-gilded flesh: both ends are blind.

Somewhere (oh image, inward lion) you
twist in what frantic sharing shuts me out;
somewhere, and yet (*oh lion*) if I knew,
doors and the dark, and all that silent shout
of ecstasy, would rise against me still.
Dreams do not solve so easily: I shall stand
and search the dream for memory, until
the hunting beast bites at my frozen hand.

ADAM OUT OF EDEN

bonae
sub regno Cinarae…
(Horace)

He knew, but never saw, the Cherubim,
the Cepheid sword's excluding beltane-wreath,
or the unreal orient gate. For him,

the barriers lay within, or underneath,
his very exile. Shadows of Eden, yes:
his partner (eyes askance, and vulpine teeth)

fruit-offering in vain her nakedness;
the bird-adventurers, the live bestiaries,
that came to hand still from their masterless

thickets and boughs; and, fiercer hurt than these,
the unattainable nearness, the spoilt sight,
of all his joy. *This* world was not at ease:

what of the huge unbiddable time, the night,
terminal black of the inordinate
hunters that crept and screamed? No more the light

bond of his naming held them: how abate
the lion's thundering furnace; bear the rush
of amber fury in the tiger, spate

of wicked ivory of wolves, the hush
of dusty hatred in the snake; the grey
volcanic shudder of power – trumpet and tush –

god out of lava, behemoth? Or stay
the ring of hungry planets he saw burning
beyond his fire, wild fire that slouched and lay

and slouched and lay, coils tightening and turning?
The terrors of the darkness died at last;
but was there comfort in the banners of morning?

New paradise no doubt lay somewhere past
eventual horizons and the known;
he ventured, was repulsed, and sought aghast

the few unmannerly acres of his own.
And so: the rainless agony of the wheat,
the field's grim flesh, her grey and flinty bone

that broke the hand upon the space, the heat
of parsimonious harvest, and the red
Lilith of war upon the crops, the feat

wound of the poppy in the womb of bread.
Stun-bent with labour in the soil where gay
and wolvish thistles, the ash-blue stranglers, spread –

serried and packed and swerved, and day by day
sprang dragon-toothed, rejoiced, and were not killed –
he watched his time drop leaf by leaf away.

This cup was deep, not lightly to be filled;
but, grief or guilt, he had not known his worst:
the airs of Eden were not to be stilled;

God, who forgave him much, yet left him cursed
with memory (oh knife!), and only glass
of knowledge between him and all that first

ineffable home. That would not change or pass;
and he must watch it while, already, years
had worn autumnal strangeness, and the strass

of rime appeared an emblem. Then what tears
his brackish flowers drank, and what dark snow
of wings descended on ergotic ears!

Memorial trees fell; fountainheads ran low;
familiar dogs were blinded; sheltering rocks
wore-down to bestial shapes; and long ago

the wilderness came fissioning like a pox
into the farm he had no remedy for.
Hear yet again the horrible paradox:

if Eden had been walled or misted, or
the man himself translated to a land
where that immortal summer burned no more;

yes (in his passion of loss, his jealous and
all-impotent ache), were Eden also stricken:
nothing had been too murderous to withstand.

But hearts must wither, sense and love must sicken,
when misery beholds beatitude:
on roses, not on racks, hell-torments quicken;

that hell is deepest whence a heaven is viewed.

THE BALLAD OF THE GOOD SHIP "AGAPË"

There was a ship called *Agapë*
(Tandaradei! O gai! Wee mij!)
for seven years rode fair at sea
but sank in the Lowlands Race.

The Captain bade no crew aboard
(Tandaradei! O gai! Wee mij!)
for Eros was that lonely lord
who sank in the Lowlands Race.

The cargo was a pearl, by art
(Tandaradei! O gai! Wee mij!)
set whole within a living heart:
it sank in the Lowlands Race.

In evil darkness below
(Tandaradei! O gai! Wee mij!)
the chisel-rats ran to and fro
to sink it in the Lowlands Race.

So busy were those breakless teeth,
(Tandaradei! O gai! Wee mij!)
and thin the timbers underneath,
that sank in the Lowlands Race,

a thousand holes in the bottom boards
(Tandaradei! O gai! Wee mij!)
let-through the sea in shining swords;
and they sank in the Lowlands Race.

One rat would bear at the Captain's hands
(Tandaradei! O gai! Wee mij!)
caresses or his kind commands –
till he sank in the Lowlands Race.

Now when he called, she disobeyed,
    (Tandaradei! O gai! Wee mij!)
for she was guilty and afraid
    who sank him in the Lowlands Race.

Up the companion-way they poured,
    (Tandaradei! O gai! Wee mij!)
the water and the shrieking horde
    that had sunk in the Lowlands Race.

She trotted over tilting decks,
    (Tandaradei! O gai! Wee mij!)
bit him on lip and heart and sex,
    and sank him in the Lowlands Race.

Sour was the mortal sacrament
    (Tandaradei! O gai! Wee mij!)
he drank as down his body went
    in the black of the Lowlands Race.

But happy she, swum safe and free
    (Tandaradei! O gai! Wee mij!)
from that dishevelled ship while he
    lay drowned in the Lowlands Race.

THE HAUNTED HOUSE

(Hommage à Thomas Hardy)

Once I lived here: the furnishings
I found so lovely, are the same.
I trespass now: the mistress brings
a dearer face, a different name.

It is no comfort to me when
I watch them at their play; but she
has always had a way with men;
and why should she remember me?

She does not. Yet their drinks turn sour;
there is a knocking in the wall;
they wait on edge for half-an-hour –
but never think of me at all.

Oh certainly, they feel no guilt;
there *is* none; but their bedroom floor
bears one square foot where blood was spilt
and, scrubbed in vain, is scrubbed no more.

Their curtains billow (that is I)
and there are corners where they freeze
whatever clothes or coal they buy.
Whom do they blame for their unease?

Behind their wainscot, where the noise
of knocking is: how can they fail,
for all the firebank of their joys,
to think of bones, and guess them male?

When toward for love their secret door
(that bars not now, nor shelters me)
gapes at them like a silent roar:
what is the shadow they half-see?

How can they fail to know the place
is haunted? – and that in between
the flesh and flesh, the face and face,
another will be, is, has been?

If I disturb their love, that is
the helpless mischief of the ghost:
once I enjoyed what now are his:
join me, my friend, and cap the boast!

What I am, you are to become;
and meanwhile, I will tell you this:
although my loving lips are dumb,
or sough because they cannot kiss,

never imagine that you own
more of this messuage than do I,
while mine is that alert of bone
and mine the stain that will not dry.

NOTES TO A MYTH

What the unicorn said –

'*The*': end of number; all definitive
short word. No, not renewing like "the Pope";
specific, like "the Lion". But: "Alive
there is one unicorn – and no more hope".
Pride, then ("the Sun", "the Devil")? – and with scope
for *I am That I am?* No: such a boast
is ash in the true anguish of the ghost.

No-one remembers, or would guess, the days
when fresh Arcadia rang with floods of white
innumerable us; a gentian-blaze
of eye and fury in that blizzard; a light
like storm on armour, splintering from our flight
and ecstasy of hooves; colossal thorns,
outblading the wild pastures, our flung horns.

None would have guessed those gale-dishevelling herds
mortal: can seas be censored, grains ungrow?
Is there a mantra for abolishing birds?
A down-clock universe – "hold in your hand, and blow"?
A long day's curfew crippled lizards, though;
yet we, ten-maring, felt the narrow breath
(when twos presented), not the bite, of death.

Clitoris-horned, our mares, grown mirage-hot
(therefore, perhaps) for zebra, horse and ass
and all bare-browed. Leahs and Rachels – not
those little running dulcimers, tinkling glass-
and-flower lutes of lechery – the grass
hushed their diminishment, then their oblivion:
and we must breed from Rahab, or from none.

Oh, but the harlot! To be counted hers!
We did not mount. And so the monsters bred –
zebras monocerots, two-horned onagers,
bizarre and puny throws less horrible dead:
and they died soon. But nothing came instead,
except our aging, our subtraction, and
a folly that was fatal. Understand:

no virgins past the teat, a fester of
ephemeral hybrids where the matrons lay
by shudders of impotence in our stallions: love,
and stark desire, found-out a twisted way.
Oh damsels in the fountains' disarray,
naked and white as we, should we have known
your pure and alien flesh would fell our own?

Bird-subtly out of thickets, the wide lawn
their voted cloister, we would peep, appalled
to feel (but rule) the rigour of the faun.
They knew our presence, though; and if they called,
gentler than snowflakes on an emerald
we would approach them, trembling, horns abased
before a joy so beautiful yet chaste.

Then we were taught they were all sovereign,
those horns, that, only dipped into the pool,
they gave elixir against age and pain,
amnesty from unease. In the mild school
our nymphs had lured us to, the virgin rule
they kissed us to, how should we grudge at all
the symbols of what made us animal?

Not without pain does keratin saw-through,
nor its pink-jelly lining; but we bored
anguish corollary with loss, our blue
eyes tearless. "Only wonder and adore",

we thought, "for, being pure, we need no more".
Yes? But the combats of the flesh are fierce;
now we could spurn, indeed, but could not pierce.

Love, do you understand? Nothing but that,
nothing but that, though barren, lethal, bent
by the deviant gravity the mares begat:
released into the nymphs' clear firmament,
its nova-light must outrage on till spent –
in which our planetary conscripts' death
was prompt and sure as gnats' in dragon's-breath.

Hate, the known murderer, is a suicide
as well: burn strongly, and the dark is sure –
yes, even love's, yes, even love's: we died
of that fire. I have days to live; and your
one hope is this: cold only will endure.
"We must love one another *or* die"? Understand:
where alone *we* could love, the word is "and".

BEAUTY AND THE BEAST: UNOFFICIAL VERSION

But I know better, whom she jilted for
that rug of lust and fang and violence
(ape-slouching ape-furred satyr-minotaur).
Charity ravished her, and rose-innocence;
and I forgave the glory that I lost;
though not the kingly lies that sheltered her
– as: "happy ever after" (gold-embossed
with dowry and cradle, crown and trumpeter).

Pictures? Why not? But *I know*. Windowless
in the stone grave-thick walls of the King's keep
there is a Glamis Chamber. Can you guess
the pity of it? That is where they sleep
and copulate, and feed, excrete, and brood
– watered and foddered naked, with no light.
And chained there to a goblin solitude.
A truth too vehement for common sight.

But *I* saw – Peeping Tom, and eavesdropper?
Shamefully? No doubt – but I *saw* that kiss
the heralds boast exchanged by him and her.
And did not like the sequel. It was this.
As fabled, now a spell-struck denizen
melted its fleshy jail, and limb for limb
gender was match to gender: yes: but when
their lips met, it was she that grew like him.

A VILLANELLE IN COLD WEATHER

So much to share, adore, and bless:
so much unreason to commit:
oh, teach me love in quietness.

Oh flower of self-born distress,
oh sun I live-in, can I quit
so much to share, adore, and bless?

Love's opal and unasking dress:
in quietness accord me it;
oh teach me, love, in quietness,

that is not less that postures less.
Teach me the dances that befit
so much to share, adore, and bless.

Goodbye to hell and hope and guess
and breathless wit outrunning wit:
oh teach me Love, in quietness.

To whom I-oblate re-confess,
on whom the burning emblems sit
(so much to share, adore, and bless):
oh teach me love in quietness.

LAST POEM

It was from dusk of pain they spoke,
the voices, high and merciless,
rung on your mercy till it broke.
How could I silence what they said?
I made them – with the bitterness
of evening bugles for the dead.

They were the souring of such praise
as blessed the wonder whence it sprang.
Oh sunlight of those eager days
all embered now; song now that swells
in flocking shadows, with the pang
and hunger of child-haunting bells!

Love's darkness, cover-up my face;
oh love that will not die, shroud still
my cenotaph my dwelling-place;
cry all that I shall hear again –
a midnight message, far and shrill
as the unseen the passing train.

VACUUM

It is time now to peel the wallpaper,
look at the off-white naevi, remember
old maps (*terra recognita,* though); lose colour
impressed for liking or by the adventurer.
There was a sea: the ashes of scale and breaker,
no Trades to plume them, blanch like talc together.
Once the world had seven roofs: no shelter
now but for anchorets of uncounted vapour.

Time to scour the terrine, gluttonous lover
(crystal? Seal the lid, then), and earn your supper
pumping it empty: cordially. Ghost-ether,
one to quadrillions, is too rich a matter.
There was a city: its golem of invader
lifted his vizard and was empty armour.
Dimensions did search outwards, the passions of number;
null both ways, now, and the hands feeling neither.

There was a sung creed: fingernail, black finger
scratching, the neumes are peeled from the psalter.
Once a thought would coral in image-water,
polyps of speech: now the racked reefs are lunar.
High time for pleating phrase into word into letter,
serif to point, and that pulled outer-inner
through itself, leaving the absent conjuror
nothing between his no-gloves but horror.

PART TWO

MYTH AND SYMBOL: THE RIGHT TRUE END

DOMESTIC ANIMALS

Clouds against air of gold
the symbols freeze and glance:
his tender limbs uphold
the banner on the lance.
There blood and silver lie
as flames within the flame
of one tall eastern eye,
the morning of the Lamb.

By soil and ash of light
he summons and prevails:
despair is in his bite,
shame in his onyx nails.
Roots of all risen trees
go down into his power:
no image but it frees
the Dog and his dark hour.

Through the furtive heat of grass
or patency of snow
his vestiges will pass,
his dangerous midnights glow.
Colder than wells they burn,
beyond all amnesties;
relinquish and return:
the Tiger's ruining eyes.

Times of the heart and will
bring each their avatars:
beasts of the field, that still
are our familiars.
Whatever forms descend,
landscape and god are one;
our victim is our end
and our companion.

He spares that threatens most:
the Tiger walks unfed;
when evening nets the ghost,
the Dog is not for dread.
Safe on the golden field
their dances break and flame;
their wounds are never healed:
the sharp feet of the Lamb.

THE BALLAD OF THE APPLE-THIEF

The apple-thief grows old and dies;
they bury him within a hill;
his body burns the grass and dries
the earth to bone; with steady eyes
his own bone face looks upward still.

So long in this bare hill he stays
that like an hourglass rib and limb
run into dust: he still displays
his bald smile and bony gaze;
but nothing more is left of him.

Now on a troubled morning these
must throb like hearts in the hill-breast:
the shrinking thief looks up and sees
threefold the roots of appletrees
piercing the darkness towards his rest.

And all his thievish senses wake:
he smells the brother-thieves above;
can bite the blood that comes to shake
his ashen hovel; hears the ache
of cruelty of homing love.

And sees the triple boughs, on each
one apple hanging; envies those
with resolution and with reach
to pluck them; longs for living speech
to tell them why an apple grows.

But he is dust and he is bone
and he is dumb and full of dread
to feel himself no more alone
and that his poisoned earth has grown
the very fruit on which he fed.

Orchard and vineyard now arise,
and valiant wheat, where he decayed;
the petalled birds of paradise
breed in the grottos of his eyes;
and in his mouth are olives laid.

THE BALLAD OF THE JOINER

The joiner looked; and not a line
to hint of the child's being his.
Then, *Beautiful but never mine*
he said, and *Who the father is,*
when tales of angel and of dove
are laughed away – now, who can tell?
But oh my love and Oh, my Love:
was this done well?

She said, *I have not done you wrong;*
but warmth of grain and animal,
and strips of linen, will not long
preserve him: see, he is so small
that were we either guilty (and
we are not) merely pity could
have seen him, by your easy hand,
cradled in wood.

Then: *I will make him what is fit,*
the joiner said, *though he is none*
of mine – and wish him joy of it.
And in an hour the work was done:
the joiner brought what he had made.
And in that coffin like a toy
he and the weeping mother laid
the destined boy.

ESPRESSO BAR: LOS TOROS

The hands and the dull mouths conspire within
this orange twilight, where giraffes of shadow
check them in motion: textures of hair and skin
disguised beneath a common birthmark, mated
on ritual boards, yet all the night their widow.
Here, in what speech, what gods are celebrated
as quietly as prayer? Though shoulders lean
to secret masses and no sun, between
these painted lights, nothing is consummated.

Pinned upon stillness and perpetual dying,
charcoal on ochre walls, three toros kneel
– naming the place – even in death defying
the priesthood of their girl-thighed matadors:
moment of lies, of consummation, seal
of blood on power. Are the symbols yours,
oh nervous hands, vague mouths and mating eyes?
Are yours the raging beast, the planted thighs,
the ecstatic blade, oh blind conspirators?

THE WATER-CRUMBS

White sink, the wet cloth spread,
the drying dishes racked:
ours; left by us, intact,
for talk or book or bed.
Stay pure for me . . . Instead,
into that shriven tract
the midnight spider comes
to suck the water-crumbs.

Hispid and sepia strays
that loose eight-fingered hand
upon the porcelain; and
groping down candid glaze
finds chastity betrays:
slips, and is deodand
for the impertinence
of spoiling innocence.

How often can we know
we have been fingered by
a darkly-pubic sly
intruder who must go
deflowering to-and-fro
and, upon cleanness, die?
Nightlong? Daylong? And may
that corpse be washed away?

POLITICAL PRISONER

They set him labouring, who meant
all strength of his to faint and kneel;
but he endured, because she leant
her own smooth body to the wheel.

They stripped him naked, and they bound
with holly-branches every limb:
sure comfort against cold and wound,
her nakedness lay over him.

They held away all food and drink
but poison, tempting him towards death:
how should his resolution sink,
who lived upon her touch and breath?

They tied a rat upon his breast
for torment, having not foreseen
to whose pain he must yield at last,
her own breast offered in between.

They took her from him, and the cell
they shut him in was dark and sour:
she *was*: and this dissolved the wall,
and lit a candle every hour.

They quarried selfhood from his skull,
humanity from flesh and face:
still she stole back to him, to call
the ruined house her dwelling-place.

YES, AND BACK AGAIN

Qui part trop tôt revient trop tard
– Alfred de Musset

I *Victoria Gardens, Truro, 1919*
Gaitered against the cold, going in terror
of the dark firs taller than fathers, knowing
the height and mystery of their bird-voluble tossing:
chill growing things, fierce calling things, inhuman
world: and a child, I, small as a shoe's voice, in it.
Oh dangerous giant escalade of gardens,
all the hill's toil and at the top no comfort –
only the strange tanks, terrible as not being born;
the alien glass and, sparse in the treacly green,
red and gold that is living weed-covered web-clad,
preciously sheltered from the naked trees
and their lost voice in the wind that could blow me away.

II *Continuum*
(Cambridge 1939-59)
Rich bodied stone the small stone bedded stream
preserved and planted green of bank and bough
still honeyed by the fixative sunlight now
as then impassive and unparting now as then
memorial without promise but a theme
an inter-time or turning back again

the scape not undone but by restoration
blazoned anew as the drops change yet not
the stream the dynasties of leaf the plot
of interlacing raining or of light and never
the play the interplay gold celebration
in green white hazel theatres playing forever

on altered flesh the altering hours relight
all scattered waterdrops continuum
of river selves and city of years that come
unparted so repassing echoing and so still
the pictures though they travel yet they write
one manifold in peace of time and will.

III *Return Journey: Cornwall, 1959*

Every greeting says goodbye already;
every meeting is the last and only;
the sliding Present gives the Past new faces.

Remembered rivers die in waterdrops;
the blown dust shivers all an imaged hill;
the known field yearly is destroyed by flowers.

Time cannot hide in hastening calendars,
nor place abide on the dissolving map;
the face of Being is itself a season.

How shall we speak, when words undo each other?
Land that you seek is never there again;
and he who would return, dies by returning.

CASE HISTORIES
IV: SPRING CEREMONIES[1]
(Tristan and Iseult)

I *Invocation at Evening*
Suave white flame in the anguish of all beauty,
flower from your garments like a martyr from smoke:
now let shine, through the vase of the ravished city,
the high intangible beacon that our love awoke.

Altar of my love, but alive and oh more pale,
and smoother, than wood fresh-planed, ungrained, more tender
than poppies under noon: let now your breath avail
unvestal to my fire, and to what both surrender.

Lithe as fire, lithe as the tongues of the blown trees;
delicate as the lilacs the feather-boned-and-breasted:
loosen as they do, unbound in the soft of the breeze,
nets for its ghostly flesh, and their sweet cups tasted.

Flesh that will whisper upon mine, fluttered shield
of blood from the molten rose of the blood, and the beleaguered
tower of blood unrelieved and not to yield:
be calyx and be cradle to me, shadow-tigered.

And now lie still my love among the wild-beast shadows,
white flame casting the unlasting shade that is I:
how brief the bridal is, but long the nights that will be widows:
peace only is to remember, this to remember-by.

II *Epithalamion*
Through the soft pole of quiet of this bed
slant the transfinite cones: cages of time,
eerie unmeanings of all space, those dread

---

1 The first three of the *Case Histories* will be found in *Reading a Medal*

and overbearing multitudes that rhyme
and unrhyme round the single point; and we,
to enact their meaning, hub of all that moves,
at peace before and after proving, see
          escape itself sleeps mute, and loves.

Mute and asleep; yet all the power is there:
stark as the day's tree, vehement as the night's
fire-winded rage of stars, proud scroll of air –
the dragon soar and scroll of amorous lights –
we mimed in flesh: the whole is there, although
the fury and strangeness of the season may
divine false weather, and we do not know
          the monsters in our future way.

Question the clock, or the blood's calendar;
but you have learnt by now they do not shift:
still as basalt astonishment they are,
and answer like known poems, a gone gift.
No measure, then, for these upshining hours,
these male and warlock solstices; no chart
for the outlandish coast this flood devours,
          nor the presentimental heart.

Since, bared Andromedae, the lamp and you
stretch helpless arms against a mystery
and a wild season, let the wild be true.
Beyond our window, gale-borne seagulls cry
one clamouring message: *quia* the gulls call,
the gulls call *quia, quia,* yet they know
how we shall answer, and the missing fall
          upon *amore langueo*.

III *The Elements*
No, let the lamp shine still: what use have we
for darkness on our white and fervent sea,
oh dolphin pale warm dolphin oh my love?

Visibly play, be jewelled in this light,
shiver and lapse upon our silent wave:
while, through the curtained acres of the night,
          forlorn wings dip and slue;
and, rocking like a mother (oh my care
under the seagulls of all-rain-belled-air)
the cold lace of the harbour hushes you.

Day and the sowing of those coloured ships
upon the new-turned water; sunlashed lips
that mousled quay or headland; the strait fingers
gilding your sleep through nets: what ran or shone,
or held its burning peace, now beats and lingers
in the unfolded flesh of girl and man.
          But we have more to do
than breathe remembered air and leash the will:
pasture and lamb, be lamb and pasture, till
the cold lace of the harbour hushes you.

Deep as the built or meadowed hillsides, long
as the low-footing pines' consent and song
in the wind's arms, the stillness of the lover
the love being sealed: on these inverted skies
culver and hawk (oh dove and kestrel) hover,
twinned like a kiss, gentler than sleeping eyes:
          such quiet have we two,
such waking quiet, skin to naked skin,
that even past the lips which lock you in,
the cold lace of the harbour hushes you.

Unalterable inward flame, that sings
like the last breath of strings,
light our tired ships to harbour, burning through
darkness at last: where, blown by opiate wings,
the cold lace of the harbour hushes you.

WHAT THE GIANT THOUGHT

When I looked down, the mast of me, and saw
his tiny scend, ant-slanting, all-but-level;
when the small waving blade, a kitten's claw
whose very shadow could not span my navel,
flashed like a speck of mica: then with pity
a faintness through my blood, it seemed that I
must break that human twiglet of aggression –
or yield myself. And it was not my duty
to fall by my own kindness. Tell me why
this lubber, I, miswent in such a fashion?

All day the deathwatch beetle, its faint shock
knocking from everywhere, out of my reach,
had worked in people's voices, endless tick
of one short name. The air I breathed was speech;
and the bright gravel of that frightened crowd
crackled with rumour: with his name. Enviewing
some thick and steeple-tilting champion
to pull my nose between my knees, a sword
the size and sheen of Thames, for my undoing,
I watched the skyline until after noon.

Nothing, of course. Go home, then? I looked down,
far down, to keep from crushing underfoot
the shifting rug of rustics I knew strewn
all daisy-faced round either planted boot,
half a mile off. There stood the peeping shrill
of his defiance; and I would have laughed,
but for my fear of booming them all flat.
Would *I* lift arms against Helvellyn Hill,
shout insults up the rain, slice at the weft
of clouds? This little creature did all that.

Why? Was he truly gulled by all those trashy
legends and lies? As: that I ate their daughters,
or split their sheep, with lust; or trampled slushy
their wheat and beet and mustard; blew-off mitres
by jumping their cathedrals; blighted fields
with my long hides of shadow. *Could* he think
I used in fact the horrors of the ogre?
But there he is. Yes; there he stands, and wields
his bee-sting menace vainer than a wink,
as if it vowed the mauling of the tiger.

I knelt (and sank thigh-deep into the furrows),
and laid my thumb out flat for him to ride,
weight on my elbows, like a lover's. Arrows
began to snap like gnats about my head;
then, while I lay and ached with tenderness
for all his futile courage, all his folly,
up hand and arm he spidered; and I squinted,
and saw him on my shoulder, thin as grass.
Flea-crack him with my nail? Puff willy-nilly
to the next field? All could have been prevented.

But, think: men say that after them the ant
(or some, the rat) will rise-up to inherit
wisdom and soul and art and government –
and not by force; by slow-maturing merit.
Well: there are three of *us* in Britain, all
male, among aliens breeding to be clever:
was *that* a future upon which to build?
He reached my right eye, pierced it through the ball:
I lay and let the myriads take over:
it is by loneliness that I am killed.

NOTES FOR A MYTH

A hand thrust out of the flames, a feather-slender
white and impossible hand on a delicate arm.
No body, and no burning; still; in form
a girl's: but phantasy or salamander?
Ringless, the wrong shape, dead as alabaster,
it was not like, and yet – oh friend and sister –
by its immune acceptance of the fires,
          I knew the hand was yours.

A hand grew out of the wall, strong-fruiting flesh
more deeply rooted than the brick and plaster;
the fingers flexing; dark; in cruel gesture.
A man's, but huge as pain to seize and crush.
Blunt as an oak-leaf, knotted, bronze as thunder,
it was not like; yet, by the alien grandeur
that gave it empire over mysteries,
          I knew the hand was his.

A hand swam high on the river; slimy lustre,
as if of pearl-shell, silvering its death;
blood on the nails; on the torn wrist a wreath
of withered petals clotted, and a cluster
of drift-weed that would slowly draw it under.
It was not like; yet in that last surrender
I saw the myth and all that it should mean,
          and knew the hand was mine.

THAT SINGING MESH
(1979)

FOREWORD

Many of the poems in this book have been broadcast in Radio Three, or in its precursor, the Third Programme. None is recent, a number of them ante-dating even those in my previous collection. As the title-poem suggests, however, they are the last that I shall write (excluding translations and perhaps light verse), and the last (apart from those) that I wish to be published. I should like this to be taken as an earnest plea to friends who may possess poems of mine, in typescript or manuscript, other than these printed here: destroy them, as I have destroyed my own copies.

Epic and dramatic poems are not often suspected of being autobiographical; and I do not see why these mostly lyrical poems, either, should come under that suspicion.

Insofar as any of these poems may be found at all "difficult", there are probably three linked causes; and much of the difficulty will disappear if warning of these is given.

First is the densely "Metaphysical" texture into which disparate and sometimes unexpected patterns of thought are plaited so as to make love-poems – which is what all these are, except the last, no matter how obliquely.

In the second place, these patterns of thought are built from symbols, metaphors, comparisons, glancing references, that have their origins in (for today) an unusually wide range of disciplines: most people no longer expect poetry to be learnéd. The difficulty here lies not in knowing technical terms (which can always be looked up) but in recognising them. For, everywhere, but especially in their use, there is a network of puns and Empsonian "ambiguities" one aspect of which will usually be erotic, and all aspects of which are usually structural parts of the poem.

Lastly, the punctuation is not always that recommended by text-books. Its intention, however, is that of all punctuation: to clarify the connexions between related images or ideas, and to preclude *unwanted* ambiguities.

A few specific "knots" are unravelled in footnotes.

MOCKING THE WIND

She found my cousin mop-faced as a gargoyle,
his young spine Quasimodo'd against summer:
        "Careful!" his mother told him.
"You'll have to stay like that if the wind changes."

I will stand upright in your steady shining,
wear for you nothing but my bridegroom-smile:
        oh love, I know already
the grey-glass moment when the wind must change.

THE TRAP

Mandarins thought that any five-doored room
would call a ghost; or many; and they built
no such a gin unless they knew for whom
(nets random-cast may catch us our own guilt,
or a sea-monster. Only fool or mage
blindly constructs what is both lure and cage).

My pentacle of senses, it well knows,
and not with terror, is inhabited:
from door to door the single spectre goes,
finding no issue, because not yet dead.

It was not I who pierced the walls, or locked
(inside or out?) the spells that brought me her
– that brought her me: for the design is mocked;
the seeming prison is the prisoner.

A WASTE OF SHAME

Let it be thought, at least, that I can read
with open lids: a body is not braille.
Yes, give the blind their flower-vase, and feed
two senses: but – are flowers dark, or pale?
Let sensuous alabaster lead the hand
through joy: but – how shall fingers pierce the veil
of the uncolour of night's eyeless land?
Its glory, not a curtain, clothed the Grail.

I have kept roses pressed within a book,
memorial gifts: what could they do but die?
That is a love at which one does not look.
And, when the love itself was sour and dry,
have let them burn, a symbol I mistook,
that should have once made happy lip and eye.

CHRISTMAS AND EPIPHANY

The visible night is tall and overstarred;
cold like a ringing glass, the hound-fang wind,
its tower of echoes: Christmas; and the cord
of the old year drawn tight (my hungering hand
roving along it, rediscovering
airs first awakened in it by your touch,
then given me). And do you know how much
will shudder at the breaking of that string?

Withdraw your senses from that outward night:
the true (ten-fingered on my calendar,
ten-petalled, doubly-bloomed, within my heart)
is hidden – all that have been ours, and are,
in one calm darkness; you its warmth of wheat,
its threefold gift, its one prophetic star.

IN ABSENTIA

Flaws in the burning-glass – the heart perhaps
left empty, or a limbus wounded, or
the arc imperfect – and its virtues lapse:
its gathered light achieves a point no more,
only a wan aureola, shadow-sun.
And I have seen a watch (the escapement wried)
in helpless fever all-but-invisibly run
past any meaning, till the spiral died.

Who is the lens your presence must perfect;
and, like the glass in darkness, have no power
without your sun to focus and reflect?
Who is the watch whose motion you must keep?
A day or death can else fill every hour
with time amok, or with all springs asleep.

SEVERANCE

Dante: *Inferno,* Canto 34

Heaven wears deeps beyond Satanic ice,
and partings wider than in triple jaws:
union obeys its own bedazzling laws,
shields of the flower-hive of Paradise.
Heaven holds many that see only one
(as we two might); nor can their Gloria pause
while multiplicit radiance lives on.
What harps will sour, though, if the fire withdraws!

But glaciered rocks demand no anodyne.
Ice and aurora! When the sun-day bleeds
like a cut flower, and the lights are down
to lair of octopus, to bed-crabs' roads;
when star and pestilence awake at noon:
where is your gift? All deeps are solitudes.

INTERCALATION

Between the Old Year and the New there lay,
uncalendared, a time of amnesty:
one hundred one score hours; nor any day
asking account of guilt or secrecy.
These, lacking month and ordinal, became
their own white dominoes against sin or shame.

When change of season spooled the minutes back,
an hour became a ghost, then lived again.
Where was its place upon the almanac?
What gift was real in it, or what stain?
Better: the clock moved forwards, and a space
was opened lacking all of ill or grace.

A medicine against whatever ails!
Then let reluctance or disgust be torn
out of your calendar: the love avails,
the uncorruption dies or is not born:
if harm were meant, harm could not clutch or live
in the intercalation you might give.

TERRA INCOGNITA

Old sailors making landfall (but the tide
unruly and the wind uncertain) boast,
in their home port, of beauties undescribed.
Fog had kept modest all that skirted coast;
no matter, legends knew the hinterland:
all was a cradle of lotos, flower or fruit;
islanders gentle, jewels many, and
the strongest storm as lulling as a flute.

Or so they say; and so the maps are made.
Valleys and orchards, gardens and springs, are guessed;
even the shape, that never was surveyed,
they make what symbol satisfies them best.
Only – one thrust of conscience? – at the centre
their lying falters, their inventions lapse:
these are the woods not even thought might enter.
There are white spaces on the best of maps.

Legends are built of longing: my own ship,
wind-racked and wary, hovers off the shore
of your enshrouded island; hand and lip
know little of that Eden, guess the more;
eyes (fox-hair, elf-rose, firm and delicate wand)
map all your beauty in the veils' despite
– shine for the apples and the flowers beyond;
but fall before your secrecies of white.

THE MARBLE CURTAINS

Not the true secrecies of cups or flowers,
soft arrowheads, or garden of the fox,
nor slender paths of silk to climb like lutes;
they are still yours; a dream to call them ours:
sightless the jewels, folded the pale flocks,
arcane the orchards and their guarded fruits.

Not the true secrecies. But flesh and word
have borne a moth-call through the lilac air,
or ghost of wings, or grass-breath of a phrase
(conjectures of the tree-invisible bird)
naming by absence what is darkly there.
The nymph within the marble knew such ways:

imaging all no less denying all,
she was the mover of the shaping hand,
the life that waited on Pygmalion's lip.
Unreal till the useless fragments fall,
beauty is waiting to be sunlit, and
to ride your alabaster like a ship.

STAGE DIRECTIONS [2]

Now let your stage lie bare, the lights contract;
we know the masquers are not far away:
there is a curtain for the final act.

If we have kept the dual text intact,
no change of scene imports, and no delay:
now let your stage lie bare, the lights contract.

The cast uneasy, timing inexact?
That comfort is not least by which we say
"There is a curtain for the final act".

The songs are fiction, but the plot is fact;
there is a past that we must not betray.
Now let your stage lie bare, the lights contract.

Let the two eponyms alone compact
exchange of parts: the end is sure as they
– there is a curtain for the final act.

Oh living theatre that I have lacked,
if not between your wings, where shall I play?
Now let your stage lie bare, the lights contract:
there is a curtain for the final act.

2 In these villanelles it will be found that each repetition of the refrains has a slightly different meaning. Note especially the various technical senses in which "fire" and "firing" are used.

NEED-FIRES [3]

The most of pain is greater than its need;
but who shall draw the colours from the glass
until the firing becomes death indeed?

To snatch reluctant wings is baby greed
(lust is foundry that unfuses brass):
the most of pain is greater than its need.

Love is the fruit on which the wasp will feed,
the adder haunting clean and scented grass
until the firing becomes death indeed.

Noosed within kisses that made neither bleed,
lover and victim speak the same *Alas*:
the most of pain is greater than its need.

The born-too-early learns a bitter creed,
all rituals and sacraments must pass
until the firing becomes death indeed.

No harvest crowns the burning of the seed
that strains and parches in the dried morass:
the most of pain is greater than its need
– until the firing becomes death indeed.

---

3 In these villanelles it will be found that each repetition of the refrains has a slightly different meaning. Note especially the various technical senses in which "fire" and "firing" are used.

LIMITS [4]

What if the winches coil-up all the rope,
the tall man's toes and fingers riding on
the drums; he, raised, a secretary's M
above the rack-bed – twanged, a fiddle E?
This pain, at this point, asks a substitute.

How often lovers dream their curve is closed:
what if their love lacks focus – if their functions
produce hyperbolae? Or the least variable
be their divisor (zero alone gives aleph)
and the failed asymptote aspire for ever?

Less happy than the recusant, they lie
unbound indeed, yet never to know limits
but those of their too-mortal graph; the pain
eased by no pawl-slip, ended by no burning,
because no substitute is possible.

4 "...a secretary's M". In at least one system of shorthand, M is represented by a convex curve. The imagery of the poem is concerned almost entirely with curves, some of which converge to (or close at) a definite limit, others of which diverge to infinity – aleph. In either case, they resemble some lovers.

DEATH BY WATER [5]

Lovers will vaunt the pains of Lawrence, threaten
a death to out-flame Latimer, the sky
one fog and thunder from their throes: they lie.
Their fires are tame and captive, soon forgotten;
when the cold flesh learns comfort, souls are dry.

Air is not lighter than the vows it carries,
for the untortured living tongue vibrates
as butterfly as they: one lie creates
the Venus-trap, the words that vulcan Ares,
the folding-out of horn or ivory gates.

Gatepost or stake or tree is earth-embedded;
the lust of pyres, the airy poem, yields
to the slow seeding of the worm-bred fields.
Worm in the blood, and of the blood, be guided:
dreams and the ardent boast are tinsel shields.

The death is in the deep: the mateless ocean,
the river's nunnery, the brooding well –
Phlebas, Ophelia, Truth. O asphodel,
witness how many, drunk upon compassion,
died in the dew of one white mercy-bell.

---

5 St. Lawrence was reputedly grilled to death. Hugh Latimer was burned at the stake. The Venus's Flytrap is a carnivorous plant. Because of his adultery with Venus, Mars (Ares) was trapped in a net by her husband, Vulcan. The gate of horn is that through which true dreams issue; false come through that of ivory. For Phlebas and the ocean, see *The Waste Land*. For Ophelia, the nunnery, and the river, see *Hamlet*. For Truth and the well that is her dwelling-place, see Democritus.

BLESSING

. . .the continual dew of Thy blessing. . .
(The Book of Common Prayer)

Not only for the small blind eyes of dew,
though ever-waking, nor the rainbow's promise,
although a giant image of those waters;
nor the uncovenanted lights that wash
dark and the day in spectra, though unbounded:
not thankfulness for these alone, by sight
or symbol; but for laws that gave us them.

All the great shining of so many mercies
impurely reaches us through prism and lens
of angel-flesh or blood-of-clouds or sky-dust:
blessing is mediate, screened by elements,
flying the lanes of sense, empowered by sense:
if light is pure, it is invisible
(the dark of God): light is the eye that sees.

Blessing is mediate, even that of love:
our thicker flesh, our living dust, our white
and crimson distillations, are the world
by which it acts, unguessed without them; love
enthroned in secrecy, but love which is
a peacock wheel of stars, a moon, a morning,
a rainbow peace, and a continual dew.

PEACOCK NIGHT

Therefore the black fan, white-and-prism-eyed,
was opened, and that emblematic bird
erected over us the rest of pride.

Not in displaying darkness to be heard,
the witch-cry of his prophecy: he kept
his bleak – our amorous – council, and his word.

And so the lovers and the augur slept,
three lulling three with breath and with no fear;
and it was only light that Argus wept.

Never awaken for the dream you hear
from his upraised his mantic throat: endure
whatever nights enfold each other: dear,

the auspice of the peacock is unsure.

THE FUGUE OF POEMS [6]

Why, then, the lines of astral celebration
– sky colour, calendar and zodiac,
narrowing to the poem's needle-eye;
arrow intention bridewell-broadening
into the poem's air and mapless nation
escapeless as the prisoner's looking-back
or voluntary cell-mouse?
                                        There is "why"
even within the beds' quadruple wing
where to this dark the exceeding lovers lie.

He who has mastered manuals – flesh or speaking
be they – and the false ivory of rhyme,
knowing the spectral escalade of key,
forgoing fugue, holding most answers back
but the last unison or suspension breaking
tension upon the common chord, in time:
one such will know all disciplines in me.
Thus my auroras, drowning white and black;
sought harmonies I hear, but feel and see.

6 Both *The Fugue of Poems* and *Reading a Score* pun extensively on musical terms (fugue, answer, unison, stop, suspension, wolf, *vox humana*, coupler, swell, mode, time, etc.) and on their non-technical and/or symbolically amorous meanings.

READING A SCORE [7]

They who by February mist, by March
blue-gashing in the cold new-nippled boughs,
loved under day or under the dark brows
of sheetless night, poised their brief-straining arch
at Now of Maybe-never: by Easter grace
awhile were given time, and Time, and place.

Closed on each other's flesh as flowers close
upon themselves, how should they sense or care
when the black moth their paraclete spread there
a sparked eclipse of wings on thorn and rose?
Fires have more colour, overshaded; peace
more purity when song and cradle cease.

But instruments, as well as echoes, die?
Still, in the quiet of the fugue that failed
(the stops immovable, a wolf that wailed
the *vox humana* down, the couplers wry,
the swell unanswering), upon the score
entry and answer sang as theretofore.

So many modes in which to fail and fear!
Though all he planned as music be unplayed,
all given time be lost, all fire mislaid,
they read the printed chords they cannot hear,
move with their thought the unsounding keys, and light
with silent verse the lamps of Easter night.

---

7 Both *The Fugue of Poems* and *Reading a Score* pun extensively on musical terms (fugue, answer, unison, stop, suspension, wolf, *vox humana*, coupler, swell, mode, time, etc.) and on their non-technical and/or symbolically amorous meanings.

SYNAESTHESIA

Nipple to emerald, rose to mercaptan, hell
to the Aurora's curtains: and how far
from Re to Mi? Your sex to Satan's fell,
dew by the glow-worm to the dying star,
and Beatrice to Lilith: count the kinds,
if they are there for counting. But I see
feathers and farms blown by ill-matching winds:
nothing can differ except by degree.

Give rabies to the rose, castrate the gem,
drink the bright vacuum, burn out of scale,
open your thighs to spectra; closing them,
shut-out the beetle, snuff the linking Grail:
the paradox of species will not stand.
So, naming love or Love – take Paul or Sade
for the pure A – only the staircase hand
can teach our strings how harmonies are made.

Lock-in the rabid weasel with your flowers,
and they will breed; give me the light, and I
will make the stone a soft consent of hours:
the deepest images are those that lie.
Change as you may, the meanings can but rhyme.
How shall a bezel bite one out of key?
From animal to chord, from flesh to time,
nothing can differ except by degree.

TRIPTYCHS [8]

I *Aspects of Barbara*
That flower-born by whom the lost forgive,
Blodeuwedd, knows this other name as hers.
Thrice-universal, thrice affirmative

(alone, so being), and by no demurs
eluctible, she strings their lyre upon
the Delphic tripos of the sophisters,

returning reason for their worship: gone,
as Barbara, the lunar flesh they kissed –
grown mad as though from ivy – and the wan

sky-felspar of her bridal wine, her mist
of panic hope: she cures their drunkenness
by the clear morning of the amethyst.

The lovers' planet, bourne of their excess,
conclusion of their premisses (the Maid
and Thief) is light they only half-possess:

---

8 So called because there are three poems, written in *terza rima*, and concerned with various kinds of three – especially syllogisms. In Formal Logic, a syllogism is a three-stage piece of reasoning. There are many forms, technically "figures", each of which has several "moods", all having their own distinctive names. The simplest is in the form: All M is P; all S is M; therefore all S is P (as, for example: All cats are mammals; all lions are cats; therefore all lions are mammals). This mood of the first figure is called Barbara; and because of that name it has been treated in this group of poems *as a girl* – or as the Triple Goddess, one of whose aspects is Blodeuwedd. The names of other moods are prefixed to the second and third sections of the poem, in which they are treated (and illustrated) punningly.
Occam blade: The logical principle, "Occam's razor", that from every study or argument one must exclude inessentials. *Hampton patency:* "Hampton", from "Hampton Wick", is rhyming slang for the penis. *Charvering* and *chivving* are petty-criminals' cant, originally Romany, for "copulating" and "knifing" respectively. *Nifë* (two syllables) is the Earth's hypothetical ferro-nickel core.

buds are unfolded that our fires invade,
but vanish soon from their illusive sun;
so spirits whom she wakes are early laid

in ash of hoarfrost, all their seed undone.
Let birds then be her only avatars:
Blodeuwedd's flowers winter one by one;

Barbara's triptych is blasphemed by scars
cat-lusted on it; and the cannibal
mare, the mad sow, were banished from our stars.

But, in the tundras of our after-fall,
spare us memorial doves' wind-opalling;
spare us the cranes that will destroy us all

if they return among the mimes of Spring;
spare us the night and rapture of the owl,
Cassandra's cry upon her desolate wing.

These are the flesh that she inhabits, fowl
of her emblem: *every tenderness*
lapses in danger and the sibyl's cowl;

every death foretold is a caress;
oh Barbara, by whom the lost forgive,
love ends in love and its devouring dress.

II *Figure One*
Barbara Celarent Darii Ferio…

Continually then to shroud from us
their Persian cruelties in the forms of reason –
moods of sweet order, figures perspicuous

as triangles – they ravished our long prison
with bannered sieges of embroidered laws
dove-purring though draconic; false horizon

of amative arras. While their knives and saws
opened harems of wounds in us, their hammers
trod vineyards on our flesh, they sang the cause

in wry faburden syllogism, drummers
to their own lullaby. We were allayed,
oh truly, by such furbishers and psalmers.

All miracles are born from love (they said);
are not your agonies a preternature?
It is by love that now you are dismayed.

Vagitus fails in joy that begs a future;
dear chronicles dress bright with almanacs;
none of your spectra was a living creature.

From pride alone a man believes he lacks;
the wild fires of your pain are greed and searching;
it is vainglory chafes at screws and racks.

Charity springs beneath no miser's watching;
in its degree, the scourge is merciful;
ferio!, *then: I lash for your enriching…*

Are we less blind for lying in that school,
glossing the dangerous moods of Media,
forgoing our allies from their twisted rule,

than surely alone on the sand (andabata
tensing for net-man), masked in one triad, thus:
“all”, “all”, and A “All”: the naked Barbara?

III *The Second Figure*
Cesare Camestres Festino Baroco...

Say she had come among us a mystery –
unfound in charvering and unapt for chivving,
by Occam blade or Hampton patency:

could we have bent her to our beat of living?
How little we, though, understood what swung
our impassioned pendulum, or our forgiving

bell of good reason with its golden tongue!
We should have known her (if she took our schooling)
older than lust itself; and no less young.

She did not come unknown to our befooling,
nor daisy-thighed, nor meaning us any shame:
but she and all her sisters, overruling

our diffident hatch, fine-drew the mating-game
to Lilith-meshes of perpetual checks.
Thus, echo-name by Malabranca name,

they hung the Nine of Primers about our necks:
a sigil in the place of lauds; the orders
of reasoned service in the vast of sex.

None, in their sweet enclave, can woo his warders;
unconsummated love must kiss the bars:
no captive princes are within these borders.

Virginal scars meet with placental scars;
the sisters were Palladian of bearing:
they went in tunics, not in scapulars.

Say she had come among us never caring
for the Frome answer (bulldyke, philosopher,
pouf, or anaesthetist, or the outstaring

clergy)? *I hasten* (could we have hastened her?);
no new is good new; hells may be justly novel,
but may be neither for nor on the spur.

Yet she made all, in this Baroque sub-hovel
of shadow-life, except the hoping part –
and, but for that, what need have we to grovel?

We cannot leave her: it is she we chart
in lust-with-reason's ill geology.
But love is the huge nifë at her heart.

WITH THE GIFT OF SPRING FLOWERS

You my pavilion and my power,
by whom to sleep and wake and not forget,
we cast the seed of every flower
when your and my uncovered knowledge met:
in token of that hour,
the petals of sharp spring are valent yet.

As cold and bitter as the wine
of winter graves, and red as childhood grief,
yours be the calyces; and mine,
the symbol of the scabbards of green leaf:
true neither way, but sign
against the superstition of the thief.

Let symbols go by opposites,
like dreams, and all the dancing-maze of joy
misname itself; and thus the writs
our years may draft against us shall destroy
only the lie and its
pale worm or virus at their dark employ.

BIRTHDAY SONG

The day is not for our delight,
nor is the light what we believe;
under the lampless eaves of night,
blindly for wonder at her white,
the lover in his living sleeve
is giving more, and will receive,
than in the naked land of sight.

But many be your nights and days,
a gallery of praise and peace:
time will release, and spring will raise,
that prisoned king, who by the ways
of risen starts will know increase
until the dance the dancer cease
and the still trance of music stays.

A SONG IN G-SHARP MINOR

In my beginning is my end… (East Coker)
Teach us to care and not to care (Ash Wednesday)

Give me the only answer
that hope and sense may know;
fetter the future dancer
and singer and entrancer:
give me the only answer,
and let the garlands go.

Is care the end of caring,
desire the end of grief,
gay garment of my wearing?
Bartholomew, my fairing
is care, the end of caring,
the dry but golden leaf.

The lost are sure of winning
a Garden and a Gate;
the penny spins, and spinning
turns end into beginning;
the lost are sure of winning:
and if they win too late?

NICHT ZU ERNST

I have seen them scuttle, faces long as a fish,
drizzling dislike from their grey-paper-bag bodies,
maggoting joy and thought, styptic to flesh,
Lenten umbrellas, black-lint-hearted ladies:
but you, my pear, my birthday, my bright penny,
my window-box, my bird-of-paradise cloak,
you my aurora, you my bath of honey,
have driven them back into the wickerwork.

I have heard them talking, sour tin-whistle voices
like fingernails on slates, intending ill,
achieving vanity and their own disgraces;
their poison-spittle, though, slug-silvering all:
but you my wing, my guinea Roman Candle,
my double-century, my Book of Kells,
my Nobel Prize, my mink, my triple rondel,
have rung them silent with your platinum bells.

But, my blue-ribbon, my four-minute-mile,
my cherry-gold pagoda, my concerto,
my smuggled brandy-wine, my swallow-tail,
my Kohinoor, my phoenix, my del Sarto,
my Stradivarius, my New Atlantis,
how shall I wholly shut the door on them
who flood me like a Sorcerer's Apprentice,
and bar the bloom from the aspiring stem?

THREE POEMS FROM *DIAPASON* [9]

I *Luna*
Honour to virgins! Of the elements, all
but five are lustful, and possessed; but these,
nobly inert, viewless, ethereal,

even in heat repel the valencies
of baser fabric (base because erect
with double gender). Such virginities,

the lunar hand of pearl of the elect,
gas-goddesses, are counted soon indeed:
what of those other vestals, to perfect

whose indivisible maidenheads there breed
no parent figures? – and from whose power descends
ipse alone? Like unpredictable seed,

they flower still where number itself extends:
other, and hybrid, rabble-integers reach
beyond themselves (Aleph begins, not ends):

these are as many, though; for each to each
– as facing mirrors double and recede –

9 I had originally planned a sequence of poems of seven satirical treatments of the so-called "planets" of ancient cosmology, each poem incorporating references to the metals and jewels and other emblems and functions and superstitions associated with the planets and their appropriate gods or goddesses. Only three were completed. It may be noted that although Diana is not mentioned in the poem *Luna*, her virginity is suggested by references to the inert gases, the prime numbers, and rhymeless words. The rhyme-scheme of each poem is circular, to suggest the (traditional) planetary orbits.
Flower still where number itself extends: The number of prime numbers is infinite – as, probably, is also the number of transfinite numbers. *Rare in your transits, etc.*: Venus has the highest albedo (co-efficient of reflected light) of all the true planets, but is only a dark spot when seen crossing the face of the sun – which happens only at intervals of 8 years, 235 years, and 243 years.

must correspond. Not so the forms of speech:

honour to those for whom there are decreed
no proper mates, whom charts of rhyme reject.
For months of iron may be paired at need;

never the iceberg plinth, or insurrect
sistrum of wyvern dogma: silver keys
that open mirrored nothing, nor connect

with any ward. Here fertile numbers freeze
as well as primes: few that are cardinal;
most, that name place or that assign degrees.

And, all being virgin, honour to them all!

II *Venus*
The Song of Solomon 2:5 (Authorised Version)

With flagons of what metal? In the bloom
of copper, transubstantiate wines must bleed
thin as the milk of garnets – knowing whom,

oh Cyprian, their shell is named for. Feed
on apples of what colour? On the bough
all gold and flame; but lusted for, untreed,

of bitter emerald. The lover now
eats without comfort, drinks and never slakes
– your goblets too turned-green. Oh Cyprian, how

flourish on fables when your power breaks?
– on paradox and horror and nightmare bride:
testes of toadstools, hag-sperm, hair of snakes,

or sweat of beetles? Yet your power died
from hope withheld: not like a dish let fall,
but like a priapism unsatisfied.

Rare in your transits, have you thought at all
by hidden sunlight your albedo wakes,
that riding past His face grows dark and small? –

all the long shining while the lover aches,
ends in a blemish on Apollo's brow?
Ancient your empire, narrow your mistakes,

but you have no more damsels to endow;
the hands that flattered once are hooked in greed;
the wells are poisoned, and the steeples bow.

Dry nipples are the grapes your kisses knead;
Hesperides, as withered as your womb,
upraise the maggot in the cups of seed:

rose, you are sour: let the sweet nightshade bloom.

III *Sol*

How is it with you, around Helicon,
deserted poet? Are they to your mind,
these groves and streams, the Muses being gone? –

all but the lying Clio and the blind
Urania. Forget those golden wires
that no more shiver and spell within your vined

academy, nor kindle from your fires.
Apollo, neither prophet nor who sings,
poor little shrewmouse of abandoned choirs,

your vatic hymns gnawn into mutterings,
your topaz chariot in the deep and cone
of annular eclipse: the chords and springs

of the fine fountain are no more your own,
your dawning dwindled to a corposant,
and your new-pubic Daphne a dry crone.

After its nuptial flight, the fallen ant
walks tunnelled earth, has loved its last of wings:
thus with your aery horse; now he must pant

– gone in the wind, spavined and thrushed – on strings
twisted or shrunk: for shame to his dead sires,
a gelding, glandered. Ride him now? That brings

no more Aeolian madness in the gyres
of middle-aether, bird-and-blaze-entwined:
true laureates are mounted on entires.

God of the broken music, the dead rind
of manhood, have you wreaths to rest upon?
Bowman-avenger paled, oh light declined,

dark be your comfort around Helicon.

DOUZAINS

I *Yeti*
Shake out your dragon streamers; autumn the snows
with balefire, link, or demon thurible;
strike-up the horrors of the horn and gong;
shiver my citadels with incantation;
and do all this in fear of me: with cause.

You have not seen me: pugs or slides, perhaps;
entrails and skins of the mouse-hare my food;
and you have heard me – or the blizzard? – crying
along the cols: but have not seen me. How
should I, your darkness made external, guilt
made flesh, old panic in my unman's mask,
submit myself a mirror to your hatred?

II *Adam (i)*
As connoisseur of the impossible,
myself to choose and name the trees forbidden,
I would have nothing in this garden altered.
A dead leaf to be pruned (or the whole suffers),
a live to bend away (and the fruit ripens);
a cherishing (eidolon of possession);
even a plaque (as: *Malus Caritatis*):
these I permit. But *o dilecta mea*,
the spoiling foxes bite at apples also;
I cannot guard against their hungering.
How to be sure (no mirrors in the leaves)
the mask that *I* present you is not vulpine?

III *Adam (ii)*
Bird in my stony garden, single flower,
dove I shall die of, rose be ruined by,
do I avenge already my unmaking?

Touches and words that spelt-out *love*: to you
are these a braille that ends in pain or pity,
a vexing as from fever-bird or mynah?

Knowing you native to the march of sadness,
I could forgive myself in your forgiving,
were this vast hand of shadow not my own
that clutches me.
                    Sweet plumage I shall never
silken again, wine-petals not breathe-in,
commend my ashes to your patroness.

IV *Parentheses*
I am not ready for the autumn (weather,
be faithless to this fallacy; St. Luke,
you shall see burned a yard of maiden wax).
But calendar and falling leaf and glass
wear the one image – happy enough did all
affections fade in the same season: how
if weathered stubble yearns for daffodils?

Turn, then, this planet penguin-over-walrus:
australe speculum. Or (since who has magic?)
cross-fold the star-map to a fair projection,
sowing the photograph and not the field,
peruking soon-bald almanacs with poems.

V *Autumn*
Fifteen, I needed no recipient
for amorous poems, nor a real object:
at most the briefly-and-far-seen beauty of strangers,
or some green Lilith only a new-learnt body.
The empty canvas and the unfleshed air
I limned and featured by the power and wish.

Fifty, the wish and power dislocated,
my portrait-gallery closed unlit, and poems
torn out of me like mandrakes: oh, the aurora
suckled in vain, is very thin and cold;
I need the cottage of the flesh, its lamplight,
its warmth of little walls, and supper waiting.

VI *October*
Do not, among the foxed autumnal trees,
wish for the lamb and hare, the parrot-green:
plays are as proud in tarnished theatres
as in the fancy's gilt and jewel-fires.
Too manifold the dancing bells of March;
I beat the steady music of the sparse
ungardens of October. Love *him-real*,
in his chrysanthemum and rowan years,
that winter must inherit, and the ice.

Oh let him understand his shortening light
is yet sufficient for the ends of peace;
his cold-roofed evening, cradle to your sleep.

VII *Last Supper* [10]
Male spiders must not be too early slain. (W. Empson)

Your elder sister, with a swallow's flight
already in her fury, the willow-slayer,
suppered her king-deceiver upon flesh:
his last meal, human; psalm her, nightingale.

The paschal coven, breaking lamb for Lamb,
drinking the scattered lintel-blood, consuming
(as He consumed) the Man soon to be Fish,
could never eat again their present symbol.

I have spun poems out of time and flesh,
webs I would have you lie on; if I come
offering these, they also are my seed:
allow my love, then: sup not yet, Arachne.

10 King Tereus violated Philomela, younger sister of his wife Procne. Procne cut up her son Itys, which means *willow*, and gave him to Tereus for supper. Eventually Philomela and Procne were turned into a nightingale and a swallow, respectively, and Tereus into a hoopoe. Looked at sardonically, the Last Supper foreshadowed a cannibal meal, and was a coven because there were thirteen present. The fish (like the lamb) is an emblem of Christ. For the Paschal Lamb, and blood on lintels, see *Exodus* 12, 2-8. Arachne was turned into a spider, in some species of which the female devours the male after copulation.

VIII *The Muse*
The true terrors of Muses – flesh that kills
by single contact; purpose unreadable
before the final revelation; mouth
by nature fastened upon *all* – not these
I think to learn from you. But even if these,
I gladly abandon guard: how else be sure
I see you in the full-moon's danger?
                                                            Yes,
that I have learned already; but not from you.
But not from you. Yet. Then I ask you this:
eating me, eat me gently; dismissing me,
dismiss me kindly; for I do not need
pain to confirm in me the nature of darkness.

IX *Writing on Glass*
I grave in diamond upon looking-glasses
(across my own, my name; on yours, my poems).
The white script overlays our living features,
reads in their absence, holds till the mirror breaks.

Windows I dare not ruin with graffiti
– not my own, even; and *your* panes look outwards
wider and oftener. By this frosty weather,
from the cold sill I write on them in crystals;
how rarely from within, and then on breath.

Keep, love, the weather cold – giving me honour
that through the unvapoured looping path your vision
may yet be clearer than through shrouded glass.

X *The Cheque-book*

Opening my account, I took their pamphlet
of twenty-four cheques all presentable
if I could earn or were I given; all
not limiting, yet, the powers of my credit.

On eight my writing was illegible;
one I forgot to sign, and one misdated;
one spoiled and threw away; too many squandered;
with four, perhaps, drew currency enough
to keep from starving; only two, I think,
were stolen and repudiated. One
was not presented.
                                        Down to my last I come;
but, being overdrawn, how can I pay you?

XI *Four Rooms*

First was a window: Xanadu and Y Brasil
beyond it, rainbow-real continents;
custom and old hope statured like the ant.

Second, a gift of boughs: being in secret
quieter than a doll's-house, happy as grass,
dark as the calling odours of the moth.

And third, a city gate thrown wide: the gentle
invader needing no destruction, trust
of the hearth and flesh disarming as the sunlight.

Fourth was an altar to the sound of bells:
an only two, untouched; but on that altar
custom and old hope staring, still alive.

XII *Lazarus (i)*
(*Luke,* 16:19ff.)
Lazarus, fainting at the rich man's doorstep,
saw the delights that epicure commanded
(as: phoenix-breast, the tongues of paradise-birds,
kebab of Colchis flamed on dragons' quills,
the flesh of unicorns) – and saw great panniers
pouting with broken meats: what Dives cannot,
servant or beggar shall not, swallow-up.
But anger, no; and hatred, no; nor envy:
the pauper understood the prodigal –
that some wealth may be squandered but may not
be shared; the very crumbs acquiring voice
in protest against glory delegated.

XIII *Lazarus (ii)*
I cannot wish the Dives from whose banquet
myself am jalousied, the parabolic
envy, despair, and flame: why *should* he feel them?
– or I attempt the Heights of Abraham?
He shall have all the water that he will,
after his human sacrament. For I,
crouched in the portico of the waste-panniers,
taking my comfort from the tongues of dogs,
reserve two prides he is not rich enough
to purchase: I can live in lack of all
he is fed with; and it is I who celebrate
(vicarious poet) *his* mere happiness.

XIV *Errors*
Should have been window, have instead been prism:
love is a white beam; I have scattered it.

Should have unjewelled; but kept on my opals:
love is the clear skin; I wore necklaces.

Should have breathed air, but was amazed with perfume:
love is to live-by; I have made it strange.

You have breathed into me, and that air is pure:
my poems add the groin and offered incense.

I have had your sigil on my heart all night:
the gift has entered me as tender gold.

Oh my impossible and lovely glass,
I should be drunken, or give *you* pure water.

PICTORIAL CALENDAR [11]

I

Tapiola (Sibelius) [12]

Castor fiber losing one chisel-tooth
dwines of the opposite whose dentine, rebutted
by no Pollux, grows giant and retorted:
a matchless liberty that seals the mouth.
Worse; for the bent continuing of that growth
returns into its origin: unmated,
now the skull-biting prodigal, self-reinserted,
enters his brain-sty and lodges there till death.
Love will bite stiffly, but you may feed and cry
while its twin gouges too; and will not die
from ivory obsession, its point being paired.
But, gnawing upon nothing, look about
for chance or strength to wrench the killer out:
breaking your mouth so that your life is spared.

---

11 As the title suggests, each poem in this sequence describes a situation or a landscape associable with one of the twelve months. Equally, the "picture" of each sonnet symbolises a specific human mood or experience. The subtleties of the sonnet-stanzas are those of musical works. Sometimes the title is only verbally, or seasonally, appropriate to the matter; in other cases, the mood or content of the music is also relevant to those of the sonnet and/or of its month. The sequence as a whole depicts an unhappy love-story.

12 *Castor fiber* is the zoological name of the European beaver.

II

Oiseaux tristes (Ravel) [13]

There have been birds, though, all the winter – parched
anxieties over the peaked rare fox, the acres
corrugated as roofs to ring-on. Mockers
or pleaders, living on luck or hate, they have searched
the hopeless, found the all-but-useless, weathered
the whittling sky, the ogham of their tracks
ollaved on snow. Bland airscape soon, and sex,
and all the bonewood parrot-fluffed and feathered.
And then what will they do? *Saynt Valentyn*
that art ful hy on-lofte, not for your sake
their Burke-lipped wooing in the procreant green,
their more than human heat, their parenthood:
change has not changed them, not will suns unmake
the chill and mood of their ancestral blood.

13 The middle English quotation is from Chaucer's *Parlement of Foules*: It was believed that birds began to choose their mates on St. Valentine's Day. *Burke-lipped* combines "hare-lipped", the murderers Burke and Hare, and the orator Edmund Burke.

III

Egdon Heath (Holst) [14]

A rock lay in the weather on useless land:
one grimace (of a self neither forced nor chosen)
without an echo; and one gesture, a hand
once-for-all clenched upon *This* – chronic and frozen
but not into pain or patience or joy; into holding.
Only the shape was insurrect, and screamed,
only the minerals tolerant of unmoulding.
Can a stone sleep? Never believe it dreamed.
What Throne, then, moving over the desolation,
breathing the scarves of mist, bleaching the sun,
printed this atony like a careless thief?
– that single instant grip of incarnation
leaving the rock awakened and undone,
pear-bruised-and-spurted, wrenched as a winter leaf?

14 A Throne is a member of the third Order of Angels.

IV

Bushes and Briars (Trad.) [15]

The hard blue the cloud-herd Aeolian wind;
and the trees baby-bald, waving like mongols:
I know the month's mind: now through bushes and
through briars (oh deciduous taiga-jungles!)
the flex-life and the winter-torpid flesh
are to be sucked and burning forth be hunted.
The oldest way to suffer is to wish;
the cleverest loss is when the wish is granted;
Aeolian then sometimes I am uneasy:
acts will exceed, there will be too much sun
to shelter from, the breastless rose turn blowsy,
imaginës revisit one by one,
discorded limbs rebound to locks of time
unkept unkeyed unkempt, the lipping-game.

---

15 The quotations are from the folk-song *Bushes and Briars* itself – the tune of which is in the so-called Aeolian mode. *Imaginës* (four syllables) is the plural of *imago*, and is a complex pun upon psychological and entomological terms.

V

Le Réveille-matin (Couperin) [16]

Well, but the clock at least was vigilant
– duenna-face, duenna-voice, with tongue
to wag the scandal of the seconds. Blent
caduceus-like together, lost among
their love, their bodies, and the lancet noon
beyond the curtains, time a Möbius tape,
they spared no senses to the chaperone
who threatened all: the cup was theirs to keep.
And tick by tick the clock was filling it;
honey and quinine drip with the same noise,
and who were they to wonder which was here
– their mutual tongues being what they tasted? Not
till the rim wept could they challenge her
who mixed her own secretion with the bees'.

16 *Möbius tape*: a strip so twisted and joined that it is endless and only one-sided.

VI

Les Noces (Stravinsky)

Under consent, intention, and with colour
of unchosen jewels – and the rite
of gathered flower-heads that kiss the culler,
the moving petals that are tilled by right.
Under delight, the auditor, the idle
autograph set firm in figures, ward
of the wet portico the rocking idol,
and the impasse where only space has warred.
Pattern of author of strait anguish; praise
of the eventual not found emotion
on which the answer not the question preys;
fish that are older than what ails them; ocean
that cannot fail and is not filled: unmanner
now unmade; rhyme in the making manner.

VII

Jardins sous la pluie (Debussy)
Der Gärtner (Wolf)

Let the twin ivies creep, antler your spiders,
over this white bough, on this web of sense;
there is nothing to be ravished that Invaders
Eponymous have not; captured, that pretence
if no more did not; king of the rosy adders,
built cobra-bolt, invest though your immense
for unseen empire of the covert riders:
summer's temptation and of Providence.
The fated standards flourish over sour
warrens of ant and worm, the sceptres dip
their sorcery to the baths of colder kaisers;
still, virtuous foxglove, yield that cordial flower
in the consensus of the parted lip:
open your lovely bite, my soft scissors.

VIII

Daphnis and Chloe (Ravel)

In this high scrubland, wether-cropped, bleak-thistled,
ferment of bees and sun, cool-ribboned air
wafting wild apple: these two rested here,
over the tolerance of the sea; blue-castled
by their solitude; their bedroof tasselled
with cotes of cloud, with fountaining birds, with fire.
Such miracles in their sensual theatre,
vainly the lemur mewed, the locust whistled.
Truly, such miracles: one relenting breast
laid bare to drink his body through the palm;
their double flesh, quick as a wound with trust;
calendars drugged and smiling; and, in this womb,
the long thoughts of night: night comes at last,
and would it be on their side when it came?

IX

In diesem Wetter (Mahler)

Marram and bent-grass; lion-coloured gale
rampant among the hornets'-mist of dunes;
running northeast, a sea curled-axeheads: fail
if you can, faith, in this desolate womb of rains,
for it is reaving weather; and the streel
of desperate clouds, grey panic arch that spans
your aisle of absence, holds no rest at all.
Fail if you can. But while the hurt remains,
you have your proper food; and that will grow:
no shore too sandy for its brackish blood,
air too enormous for its knitted root.
What idle and exalted scrolls of blue,
arcadian sun, or sweet-lake-whisper, could
so breed endurance? And so vise the heart?

X

Preludi autunnali (Malipiero)
Eye-coloured sea, together we read your turning
sun-leaf in Kufic, and your minstrel sheets:
was there no other message than height and morning,
no flux to silver of your carol of lights?
This was the summer birth: no granite awaiting
memorials, beyond the twofold cradle,
no golded letter tarnished? No room for doubting
your glitter of slow chisels was not idle?
Oh harbour-coloured eyes, what are you seeing
now the sung leaf is turned, or torn adrift,
the sistrum-light of water stilled and greying?
Bruise-blue of shadows; one small yacht beginning,
under the predatory wings, to lift
October sails, and run where the day is running.

XI

Petrushka (Stravinsky)

Till now, to others: when at last it happens
it hurts less finally than the dolls believe:
the hand that held the puppets falls and opens;
the puppets twist, and rise, and are alive.
But now they can no longer move together –
though (look) the strings are tangled. The freed limb
searches for muscles to replace its tether;
the muscles have no music ruling them.
But up, slack-sinewed; and a kind of bow
(no longer to a fellow) to the mirror;
then, out of habit, part of the old dance.
Look once around no-longer home. And now
learn that your world had edges; and, with terror,
stare out across the waiting audience.

XII

Des pas sur la neige (Debussy)

Fold back the snow that haunts us: mantelpiece
and threshold, chimney (all the symbols lie)
are frozen; the wing-burning marigold eye
that lit our cradle will not will release.
Loose the lost summer that may not increase.
Loose the lascivious ivy's fingers, high
on the harnessed oak; loose our enclosing sky
to us, and in the sky its troubled fleece.
Granted, the snow bears footprints: something passed
and, out-of-sight beyond, gapes dead, or hides;
but that was gales ago, and is the last.
What moor from valley, tree from tree divides –
paled always – now is hugged into a waste
that nothing viable, falcon or fox, abides.

THAT SINGING MESH [17]

I planned for poems to be dressed in steel
and spider's-lace of harpstrings, that the flesh
(its nakedness unseen to pulse or feel)
dance under spectra in that singing mesh.

I grew my orchards with no living fruit:
poems were trees of wind-hung prisms, each
bejewelled like a grotto, the quick root
stalagmite-risen to stone plum or peach.

Time to shed filigree and crystal for
the naked body and the bitten drupe;
maze-music now, and rainbow-glass, no more,
but the high bird and the clear-polished loupe.

Now my faience and hippocras of rhyme
are shamed by peace of water and of delf;
the poet-archer tramples (it is time)
the poem-python that encoils itself.

This was the last root fertile, and this tree
shall bear its prisms too. But these are all:
and the last music in the sky shall be
a breaking string; and then the axes' fall.

---

17 *A breaking string, etc.* In *The Cherry Orchard*, Act Two, there comes from the sky the sound of a snapped harpstring – a symbol of approaching dissolution.
The poet archer, etc. Apollo, god of poetry, who killed the great Serpent that lived in caves on Mount Parnassus.

APPENDIX A

POEMS BY SARAH TILLER

VESPER

Half-past eight on a late summer evening,
and the heat seeps out of the day;
scents intensify as the light fades: a waft of roses,
the sour-yellow smell of hay, the warning tang of nettles.
Already the long grass is cool and dank under the trees
where midges hang in muslin swarms stirred by eddies of air.

At last the danger of wasps recedes,
but moths and crane-flies are flexing their wings;
homesickness nudges, and darker things
stir and begin to bite.

Perhaps the shade of an insect
carelessly crushed underfoot
will summon a vengeful army of its kind
to pour, singing with rage,
through the bedroom window.

Or the ivy which corsets the trees
will release its hold, and dance
across the lawn on pentacle leaves,
blind tendrils groping for a warmer prey
to constrict with its dark-green malice.

Or one of the trains which run
along the ridge above the farm
will leap ungoverned from the tracks,
swift and unaccountable as adult anger,
and hurl its devastating thunder
down upon the house.

Inside the house, someone switches on a light;

bats emerge from the eaves and speckle the pale sky.

ALCHEMY

Once I believed the scavenging muse
at my shoulder, when she licked her lips
and hissed, "All deaths belong
to us; the base metal of pain
may be transmuted into golden song.
Listen."

And we heard,
she and I,
the sizzle of an insect
as it butted a hot bulb;
the minuscule thud
as it fell.

She smiled,
my muse,
and said, "Smell
the charred, brittle flesh.
Tell me what this one
tiny death may represent."
I tried: I trusted her then
and I tried.
Much later we learnt how swans
may, in the dark, mistake
a rain-washed road for a river;
they try to alight, and die
with no time for a final song.

My muse bared
her jackal teeth
and whispered, "Yes!
We shall sing instead.
We shall feast
on symbol and gorge

on metaphor; think
of confidence misplaced,
of wild hopes that sink
like kites abandoned by the wind;
see the glittering filigree
our alchemy will forge."

But I pictured it too plainly
in black and crumpled white,
stark as a woodcut pinned
to a gallery wall: Landscape
with wet road and broken swan; night.

BREAKING IN, BREAKING OUT

What should we find if we cracked the shell?
New worlds dazzle the unaccustomed eye;
The prisoner may learn to love his cell.

When actors deceive and do it well
Enough to give reality the lie,
What should we find if we cracked the shell?

The poet's enmeshed in his rhythmic spell,
Lonely as the sun in a cloudless sky —
The prisoner may learn to love his cell.

What of the heaven that you foretell,
You priests, and the god you daren't defy?
What should we find if we cracked the shell?

Surely the saints must secretly rebel:
The road too steep, the hill too high?
The prisoner may learn to love his cell.

And I should leave the cage where I dwell,
A bird that sings but will not fly.
What should we find if we cracked the shell?
The prisoner may learn to love his cell.

LONGING

Black roads stretch out before me,
Where they lead I do not know;
But the roads can never take me,
Take me where I want to go.
Already I am weary, though my journey's not begun;
Black roads roaring onwards beneath a sullen sun.

Grey river runs forever,
Who can stem the water's flow?
But the river cannot take me,
Take me where I want to go.
Already I am lonely, though my journey's not begun;
Grey river, shining river, beneath a silver sun.

The sea is like an earth-bound cloud
That lunar breezes blow,
And the sea can never take me,
Take me where I want to go.
However far I travel across the swaying tide,
I shall find the same sad longing when I reach the other side.

FAQ

You doctor of the soul, head winsomely inclined,
who assured me it didn't matter what was real
(a philosophy I can't accept) – ultimately your mind
was laid bare more than mine. How does that make you feel?

You plaster madonna shedding gory tears
(Mary, why not bleed as women have always bled?),
how can you understand pain that lingers for years?
Your sorrow was short-lived, your son rose from the dead

so they say. And speaking of him, did his torment so far
exceed the suffering of ordinary men
denied the morbid glamour of crucifix or pietà?
(Just ignore the rustle of cassocks...)

But then again,
where should I turn for solace in anger, or fear, or loss,
I who have no faith in serpent-staff or cross?

DARKNESS

Once we knew what darkness meant
And, fearing it, we huddled in the light
Of candle-flames or fires, amid the swaddling scent
Of smoke and sleep and safety. Few went

Out where the shadows sought whom they might
Devour; perhaps a child wandering late
Would hurry fitfully, his home in sight,
Playing grandmother's footsteps with the night.

For the night held secrets – loneliness, lust and hate,
Poverty and evil savagely intertwined;
Pain grew fiercer then, and hungry sorrows ate
With an anger only sunrise could abate.

Now there is almost more light than we can stand:
Green, red; go, stop – above all stop and look,
Look at the food, the drink, the book,
The shop, the film, the band,
The leering face, the pointing hand,
The dancer, the winner, the goal!

So sometimes we close our eyes and seek the dark elsewhere.
And some find it almost with pride – yes, I've heard people say
"My darkness is greater than yours," relishing the grey
Cataracts of despair;
And turning to the light they dare
To celebrate some compline of the soul.

But others still understand the meaning of the night.
Their dusk seeks only dusk; and in the dark they pray
"Unmake me, Lord, unmake me: I can no longer fight
The unrelenting vigilance of light."

DUALITY

Uncertain even how to write
its name, grey must look two ways
as Janus did: towards black and white,
dark and light, the beginnings of days
and their endings. Grey is menacing and chaste,
like gargoyled churches dank with the praise
and prayers of centuries, or patience embraced
reluctantly: a pallid virtue, thin
and shifting as morning mist chased
by a riverside wind. The conciliatory grin
worn by tremulous old age to hide
the fearful frailty fluttering within
is also grey. Like man, grey can't decide
between the sewer and the sky;
for grey is mourning gently laid aside,
the softness of dust, raindrops that try
in vain to dilute the sea, a sin
of childhood indulgently recalled (or is the eye
deceived by distance? Doubts begin
their wambling waltz; the smile's replaced
by grey perplexity.) But are these really akin:
cloud and concrete, wrought iron and silk-laced
spider-webs? Such cunning displays
of opposites to intimidate and charm!
And two-faced grey, like evil ignored, stays
on and waits to be noticed, to mislead, to blight
or enchant by turn. Under its gaze
I am uncertain how to write...

INFECTION

What can it be, this châtelaine
that drags so heavily at my waist,
rattling its reminders every day?

Words are clasped to words like links in a chain,
and every image is chased
by dozens more, in a shadow-play

of abreaction. Its clinking refrain
punctuates memory, leaves joy defaced,

and rainbows daubed with bitter grey.

Why must these ponderous keys
so wantonly unlock doors
and leave them agape, leaching
the ichor of regret, spreading disease
that seems to penetrate the pores —
virulent, far-reaching,
impossible to disperse?

Keys – the very word
resembles the cry of a carrion bird
or a jailer's dying curse.

SNOWFALL

A meagre snow fell. At the station, a sign
Warned of delays on the Bakerloo line -
An incident, it went on to explain
Involving a person under a train.
And the public address said the staff at the station
Were collecting for charity: any donation
Gladly received for the young in distress...
Please give to this famous fund... Well, yes,
But this person they mentioned – what did he do?
Had he a ticket, and if so, where to?
Or perhaps he decided on risking a fine
Before causing delays on the Bakerloo line.

Official statistics don't distinguish a fall
From a leap intended to end it all:
They simply refer to "fatalities arising
From a person striking a train". It's surprising
How many do it: back in, say, '99,
Twenty-two people caused delays on the line
Of their choice. Snow falls much more rarely
Than that in London, and therefore quite fairly
Occasions more comment.

And the public address
Continued to tell of the children's distress;
Collecting-tins rattled. Still the snow fell
(Or jumped, or was pushed – impossible to tell
Really) and, striking the traffic, it died
A million small deaths in the grey streets outside
The station. In the tunnels below
Dark wheels bore their chrism of blood and snow.

RIDDLE

One-legged cyclops,
I am stark and strong;
Men seek me but daren't come too close.

In the dark I am king
And the watched-for blink
Of my single eye
Commands men's movements
And their destiny.

For some I am a home
(or maybe a prison)
And they must be
As lonely as I,
Gazing at the grey sea,
Listening to the grey gulls.

THE LAMENT OF THE UNKNOWN POET

(A Hymn of Hate)

I long to be published; it seems a vain hope
(though some of the stuff that's in print's pretty poor)
but I don't want to write like Wendy Cope.

I can't understand it: daily I grope
for the reason why she's the one critics adore,
while I long to be published, but haven't much hope.

A jingle like this is money for old rope:
I could churn out a dozen a day, maybe more,
if I wanted to write like Wendy Cope.

"You've just got to laugh," says her voice. I say, "Nope,
I'll laugh, Wendy dear, when I choose, not before."
But I long to be published, and still live in hope

of one slender volume, vast in its scope,
resonant and deep, so the press cry "Encore!"
even though I don't write like Wendy Cope;

but I just blush unseen – or rather I mope.
One thing, however, is perfectly sure:
I'd love to be published, I've almost lost hope,
*But I'm damned if I'll write like...*Wendy Cope.

WET CEMETERY

Under the rain
neglected flowers droop
in vegetable mourning.

It must take more than
normal devotion
to keep tending flowers
you can't pick or
see from your window.

So as an incentive
to cultivation
let people grow beans
or strawberries or
lettuces instead.
To "Always in
Our Hearts" add
"Something in
Our Stomachs".
After all there's
usually a waiting-list
for allotments.

Organic production methods
would be best,
though I would
discourage slugs: "Tough
on slime, tough on
the causes of slime,"
I say.
        But chemical
fertilisers would be
entirely redundant.

APPENDIX B

POEMS BY MATTHEW TILLER

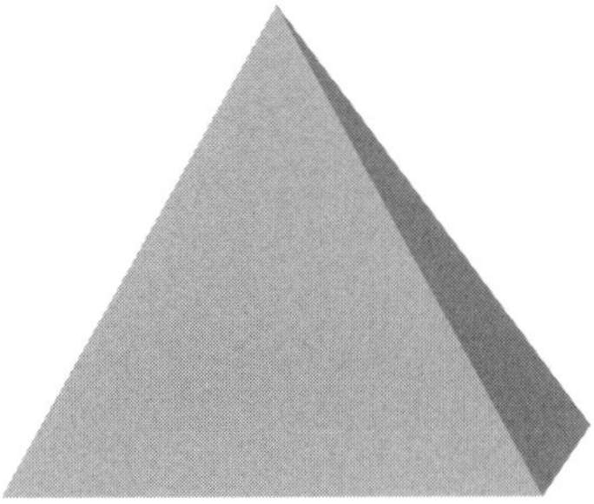

STRANGE STREAM

March's rain and sleet have sidled
Down a dry, aimless ditch
And formed a stream.
Pollution, sand or unusual mud
Has turned the water to darkest tan,
A cousin of the pale curls on the bank
Thrown aside by the trees two seasons back.
Other leaves have drowned and lie, static,
Frosted with air bubbles and grit,
As though what was once resigned to rot
Has been halted, half-decayed.

ANTICLIMAX

Along the towpath comes trotting
A dog, in colours a cat would call tortoiseshell.
In his mouth is the slim arm of a willow.

He must have chosen this stick for himself;
No master would throw something so unwieldy.

He looks like the herald of something,
Fulfilling his small role with canine humility.
There should be an exquisite procession behind him -
Chariots, or wagons overflowing with bands,
Seeming to follow but, in truth, leading.

But instead there follows a father, dutifully propelling
A resentful pushchairful of baby.
Their eyes are trained on the gravel —
Eyes impervious to trees.

SARAH

On a horse called Copper,
Sarah rides through the mist.

The horse is not dutiful, the rider is not vicious;
They share exhilaration at the soft-sharp beauty.

Through Copper, Sarah can feel the rhythm of the terrain:
The skittering pebbles, the limpet mud, the resilient turf.

For herself, she sees the mist interwoven with the brambles,
Feels upon her face the ice-fresh air,
Returns the thistles' admiring purple gaze.

Sarah takes in the morning with the now-ness of a horse.
Having felt like this, who would want contentment?
What too often brings sadness is truly worth having
If even once it also brings this kind of joy.

Sarah feels no pride for seeing what she sees,
But if the land looked in her eyes, it would envy its reflection.

THE BELL

The bell hangs untolling in the earthy brown cliffs.
Over the years of neglected solitude
It has gathered character, becoming almost human. Like a hermit,
It pursues its motionless path peacefully... but to conclusions
No mortal could countenance. It makes its own rationale
For being where it is, forgetting the eccentric
Who fastened it here in the first place.

Two men and a donkey pass by, and the bell
Tolls softly for the first time in years.
It is greeting the donkey,
And it is only the donkey that hears it.
The donkey starts ahead, pulling its rope taut,
Braying anxiously. The men do not consciously hear the bell,
But the sound edges down their inner ears
And into their brains. The faintest touch
Of the bell's philosophy
Is enough to disturb them.

And none of the three creatures will sleep well tonight.
But the bell will doze with brash confidence.

OBJECTS AT NIGHT

The daisy, eye closed,
Concentrates to overhear
The susurrant night.

A punctured football
Oozes sluggish air; its breath
Merges with the wind.

Thrown-out magazine:
Stray breezes flip its pages
For the rats to read.

An aeroplane's light
Manoeuvres through the darkness,
Disguised as a star.

Downstairs in the dark,
The clock's tick and the tap's drip
Softly syncopate.

The fairground grabber
Shoves aside silvered toys and
Scrabbles at the glass.

The gate's hinges sing
In the moon-jilted churchyard.
Only gravestones hear.

BURR

A teenage girl was walking along a wooded road.
As she brushed against a plant
A burr stuck to her jeans.

Though tabby-cat-furry from a distance,
Close-to it was a determined beast,
Clinging on fiercely.

When the girl arrived home
She flicked the burr lazily onto the hallway carpet.
The next day,

While her agitated father was searching for his shoes,
The burr hooked itself to his acrylic sock.
It hitched a ride on his instep, all the way to his office.

Midway through a board meeting
He slipped his foot out of his shoe
And managed to shake the burr off.

Later it was spotted by a cleaner
To whom the countryside was septic... and yet
It didn't seem right to throw away the burr.

So she placed it on the room-sized table,
And it lay in the sunlight as before,
Surrounded by wood, but this time butchered wood.

And the breeze whisked superfluously
Past the air-conditioned block.

HARVEST SONG

Harvest's ending; bent down in the mind field,
What are you gleaning?
Husks all over, not much to put together
Who'll catch the meaning?

Hidden rivers underground
Bleak caverns seldom found
Fragile branches, just too high
Filtered colours flee the sky (Why?)

Drowned mountains in the sea
Cypress roots far from the tree
Vapour scattered in the blue
Someone must see this anew (Who?)

An octopus as clear as glass
Patterned coats that match the grass
Let them go without a care
Magma thrusting for the air.

APPENDIX C

PHOTOGRAPHS

Terence at 2 years old

5 years old...

... and 13

more 1939

Tiller at Cambridge, 1938

ler at Cambridge, 1938

1939

Terence Tiller with Penny in Cairo

Camels going to university

Egypt, 1944

Tiller with group of students, Egypt

Tiller with cousins

1960

Sixties

At the BBC

1954